A Jacana Book

First published in 2002 by
Jacana
5 St Peter Road
Houghton
Johannesburg
2198

Copyright © Ben Trovato

ISBN 1-919931-18-X

Cover and Text design by Disturbance
2nd Floor Innesdale
101 Innes Road
Morningside
Durban
4001
e-mail:disturb@mweb.co.za

Printed by Formset Printers
22/23 Kinghall Avenue
Eppindust
Cape Town
7640

Mr Ben Trovato
PO Box 1117
Sea Point
8060
Cape Town
South Africa

19 August, 2001

Dear Mr Kaczynski,

It has been three years since a judge sentenced you to four consecutive life terms for killing three people and maiming dozens of others. I expect for you, it feels a lot longer.

As I understand it, your hatred of technology drove you to send letter bombs to people who were, in your eyes, the enemy.

I think there is a little Unabomber in all of us. Just the other day my cellphone started ringing for no apparent reason. I flew into a rage and hurled it across the room, but it went through an open window and struck a passing motorcyclist in the face. He lost control and ploughed into a delivery van owned by a computer shop. As it turned out, the biker worked for a company that manufactures automated filing systems that will one day make thousands of South African secretaries redundant. So I never lost any sleep over it.

I have also had unpleasant incidents involving my CD player (settled with a baseball bat), my digital satellite dish (shotgun) and my wife (Brenda) who refuses to cook or have sex with me. In this regard, I suspect that I have been replaced by one or two battery-operated appliances. Needless to say, I have a team of lawyers standing by in case of emergencies.

I must congratulate you on having succeeded in getting several influential American newspapers to publish your manifesto in the mid-1990s. Sure, you had to threaten to blow up New York to get them to do it, but it worked. For one brief moment, you controlled the media. And by extension, the world.

A world rapidly being destroyed by industrialisation. British textile workers had the right idea in the early 1800s. For five glorious years, they smashed machinery in the belief that mechanization would lead to unemployment. And yet none of them were called paranoid schizophrenics and thrown into jail for the rest of their lives. You are simply a modern-day Luddite who used more sophisticated methods to achieve the same aims.

Come and visit me when you get out.

Yours truly,

....
Ben Trovato (Mr)

5

TED KACZYNSKI
to
MR. BEN TROVATO
P.O. BOX 1117
SEA POINT
8060
CAPE TOWN
SOUTH AFRICA

5 November 2001

Dear Mr. Trovato:

Thank you for your letter of August 19. I have been unable to answer it until now because I have been occupied in preparing a petition to the Supreme Court of the United States. From this you can infer that my legal process has not yet been concluded.

Since you seem to assume that I actually am the Unabomber, I have to explain that my guilty plea to the Unabomb charges was the result of coercion, and that I am currently attempting to have my conviction overturned as invalid. People sometimes plead guilty without being so simply because that may represent their least undesirable alternative in a given legal situation. But I will say no more on this subject, since lawyers have advised me to avoid discussing these matters with anyone until my legal process has been concluded.

To come to the point of this letter, in your letter to me you complained that your wife was refusing to have sex with you, and you expressed a suspicion that in that regard you had been replaced by "one or two battery-operated appliances." I am happy to inform you that you need not despair. Where technology creates a problem it also offers a solution.

Scientists tell us that some day we will all be able, in effect, to turn ourselves into machines. We will be able to "down-load" our brains into the electronic brains of machines so that our consciousness – say the scientists (and who can doubt the word of scientists?) – will live on in the machines. To ordinary mortals like you* and me this may sound like a lunatic fantasy, but it is actually proposed in all seriousness by distinguished scientists. See, for example, an article by Marvin Minsky in Scientific American magazine – October 1994, if I remember correctly.

The procedure proposed by Minsky and others holds the solution to your marital problem: Some day you will be able to turn yourself into a battery-operated appliance and thereby resume having sex with your wife.

I hope that this news cheers you up a bit.

Best regards,

Ted Kaczynski

Ted Kaczynski

* I assume that you are an ordinary mortal. If I am mistaken, please accept my apology.

Mr Ben Trovato
PO Box 1117
Sea Point
8060
Cape Town
South Africa

12 July, 2002

Dear Ted,

Thank you so much for taking the time to reply to my letter of 19 August, 2001. It's hard to believe almost an entire year has passed since then. On the other hand, a year for you probably feels like a decade.I was appaled to learn that the Supreme Court had rejected your appeal. From what I can gather, your initial guilty plea was part of a deal to avoid being portrayed in court as mentally ill. Or was it a plea bargain to avoid the death penalty? I am a little confused on the details. In your last letter to me (November 5, 2001) you mentioned that you preferred not to discuss these matters until the legal process had been concluded. Can you talk about it now? I would be most interested to hear the real story.

You may recall me complaining about my marriage, and that a couple of battery-operated devices had rendered me virtually obsolete. Well, Brenda's heart remains trapped in pack ice. I suspected it might be a circulation problem and attempted to open up her veins with a rigorous slapping. Well, that certainly got her blood up, if nothing else. She retrieved my stick from where I keep it hidden and set about my lower body. She only stopped when she suspected that I was enjoying it. But I can assure you that I dislike a beating as much as the next man. I admit to once striking her several times in a bid to quell an outburst of hysteria, which subsequently turned out to be hay fever. However, the symptoms are similar and one is easily mistaken.

I am from the old school and feel it is undignified to beg for sex. Dinner is another matter. I can cope with the dangerous psychological games and petty assaults that are essential to any healthy marriage, but I am struggling to come to terms with the withdrawal of my conjugal rights. I tried approaching the Human Rights Commission for relief, but they reported me to the police. So not only do I spend every night celibate and hungry, but I also lie awake waiting for burly thugs in camouflage to kick down the door and drag me out into the street sporting an unrequited member for all the neighbours to see.
In your letter, you told me not to worry. That soon I would be able to down-load my consciousness into a battery-operated appliance and resume having sex with Brenda. For a moment, I thought you really were mad. Then I spotted your reference to "Marvelous" Marvin Minsky, a man who makes Charles Manson seem like a poster boy for mental health. He talks of using "nanotechnology" to grow fields of micro-factories in the same way we grow trees. How nice. Just taking the dog for a walk through the micro-factories, dear. He rambles on about spawning "mind-children" that think a million times faster than we do. On the old question, will robots inherit the earth, Minsky says: "Yes, but they will be our children." Do the authorities know about this man? And what has he done to George W. Bush's brain? Like you, he is a Harvard man. Can we blame Harvard?

I have to go now. Minsky has made me afraid, and I am going to hide the electronic equipment before Brenda hears about nanotechnology. Looking forward to hearing from you again.

Yours truly,

Ben Trovato (Mr)

7

TED KACZYNSKI
to
MR. BEN TROVATO
P.O. BOX 1117
SEA POINT
8060
CAPE TOWN
SOUTH AFRICA

29 July 2002

Dear Mr. Trovato:

I have just received your letter of July 12, 2002, in which you ask about my legal case. I am enclosing herewith a copy of United States versus Kaczynski, 239 Federal Reporter 3rd Series, pages 1108-1128 (9th Circuit 2001), which will probably answer most of your questions.

Please give my regards to Brenda, and tell her that I especially request that she respect your marital rights for at least one night, or, better, every night.

Sincerely yours,

Ted Kaczynski

Ted Kaczynski

tives. Three men—Hugh [...]
bert Murray, and Thomas Mosse[...]
by Kaczynski's devices, and ma[...]
[...]eople were injured, some severely.
[...]nski made what has been [...]
[...] most extraordinary [...]
[...] history of [...]
[...]halt

that affo[...]
right to [...]
under [...]
prem[...]

A r[...]
ly [...]
o[...]

seek the [...]
ments on [...]

The C[...]
to the [...]
Burre[...]
lic D[...]
Cali[...]
P[...]
a[...]

[...]der both indict-   mental state defense, to represent him.
On December 16, he received a letter indi-
[...]ating that Serra would be available, but
[...]mber 17 Serra withdrew from con-
[...]nski's counsel
[...]ters in

[...]ly as a delaying tactic after his eve-of-trial
request for substitute counsel was denied.

13. Criminal Law ☞273.1(1)

Guilty plea was not rendered involun-
tary by threat of mental state defense that
defendant did not want presented, where
defendant's aversion to being portrayed as
mentally ill was inconsistent with his willingness to allow his attorneys to introduce
such evidence later during penalty phase.
U.S.C.A. Const.Amend. 5.

Theodore John Kaczynski, pro per, Flor-
ence, Colorado, defendant-appellant.

Robert J. Cleary, R. Steven Lapham
and J. Douglas Wilson, Special Attorneys
to the Attorney General, San Francisco,
California, for the plaintiff-appellee.

Appeal from the United States District
Court for the Eastern District of Califor-
nia; Garland E. Burrell, District Judge,
Presiding. D.C. Nos. CV-99-00815-GEB,
CR-96-00259-GEB.

Before: REINHARDT, BRUNETTI,
and RYMER, Circuit Judges.

Opinion by Judge RYMER; Dissent by
Judge REINHARDT.

RYMER, Circuit Judge:

Theodore John Kaczynski, a federal
prisoner, appeals the district court's de[...]
of his motion under 28 U.S.C[...]
vacate his convicti[...]
Kaczynski [...]

in good faith, that counsel could control
the presentation of evidence, and that the
plea was voluntary, the district court denied the § 2255 motion without calling for
a response or holding a hearing.

This court issued a certificate of appeal-
ability. The government submits that
Kaczynski is foreclosed from raising the
voluntariness of his plea on collateral re-
view because he did not do so on direct
appeal, but we conclude on the merits that
the district court did not err. Therefore,
we affirm.

I

The facts underlying Kaczynski's arrest
(April 3, 1996) and indictment for mailing
or placing sixteen bombs that killed three
people, and injured nine others, are well
known and we do not repeat them here.
Rather, we summarize the pre-trial proceedings that bear on the voluntariness of
Kaczynski's plea.

The California Indictment (returned
June 18, 1996) charged Kaczynski with
four counts of transporting an explosive in
interstate commerce with intent to kill or
injure in violation of 18 U[...]
three counts of m[...]
with int[...]

Mr Ben Trovato
PO Box 1117
Sea Point
8060

28 June, 2001

Dear Deputy Leader,

I was wondering if you chaps are still going, now that Mr Terreblanche is on long leave.

The reason I ask is that my boy, Clive, is approaching Manhood and is in dire need of a little toughening up. He was showing distressing signs of confusion concerning his gender, but I am happy to say we have managed to break him as far as the lipstick goes.

Within a month of two, he will need military training. I served in 2 Signals Regiment myself, and I can honestly say that a couple of years in the SADF left me a changed man.

I heard on the news the other day that the SANDF was planning to introduce voluntary conscription. This is about as confusing as sticking an N into the middle of the name to prove that the army no longer goes wandering off into neighbouring countries.

Then I saw an interview with General Andrew Masondo on telly the other night, and I realised that if I sent Clive off to the army, one of them would not make it out alive.

That is when I thought of the AWB. I recall that you have an army of your own. Tequila, I think they are called. Do they still exist?

Clive needs to learn the meaning of patriotism. He needs to grasp the significance of a uniform (although Brenda was wrong to burn his favourite camouflage skirt – it set him back considerably). He also needs to learn the value of spending time with boys his own age. I am not sure who he hangs around with at the Institute, since parents are denied access to information of virtually any kind. However, I am confident that his so-called friends are little more than pale shadows of the strapping, courageous patriots of Tequila.

I know in my very soul that the Tequila Youth can teach Clive a thing or two. However, I must mention that he is still a virgin. I am in the process of helping him across that particular hurdle. And once his voice has dropped an octave or two, he is all yours.

Please let me know if he can make the January intake.

Yours truly,

Ben Trovato (Mr)

10

AWB

Verwysing MOS/I/7/01

22 November 2001

Dear Mr. Trovato

We acknowledge receipt of you letter dated 28 June 2001. We are being flooded with mail and although we want to reply to all the letters and e-mails right away, it is humanly impossible. Please accept our sincere apology.

Concerning your situation with your son, it is a tragedy that out sons and daughters isn't receiving the training and discipline they so desperately need. Non-the less, we can't allow them to go and die, fighting a war for countries we regard as enemies. Hopefully the situation will change in future.

The government banned military training to non-government organizations and we won't be able to assist you with military training. If you and your family can assimilate with the history and strife for freedom of the Boer people, you are more than welcome to join our movement. Membership is subject to approval.

If however you want to support our cause without being a member you can do so by helping us financially. We are busy reorganizing the movement and need financial assistance urgently. Our banking details are as follow:
Afrikaner Weerstandsbeweging (AWB); ABSA Bank; Ventersdorp Branch; Branch code: 334-539: Account number: 2250142016

Cheques or postal orders, to the above address are also welcome. Please send them with registered post.

Thank you for your support. We hope to hear from you soon.

Boer greetings

A. Mostert (Editor: Storm)
Communication Administrator

The struggle that our fathers begun will rage till we've conquered.

NR. 9   AWB NUUSBRIEF / AWB NEWSLETTER   DES - JAN 2002

Posbus 4712, Kempton Park, 1620   Tel. / Faks. (011)975-3129 / 083 206 1291   E-pos: storm@awb.co.za

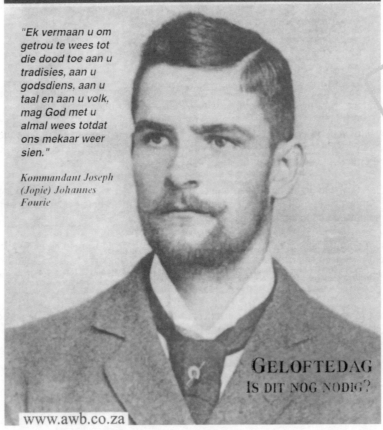

"Ek vermaan u om getrou te wees tot die dood toe aan u tradisies, aan u godsdiens, aan u taal en aan u volk, mag God met u almal wees totdat ons mekaar weer sien."

Kommandant Joseph (Jopie) Johannes Fourie

GELOFTEDAG
IS DIT NOG NODIG?

www.awb.co.za

Mr Ben Trovato
PO Box 1117
Sea Point
8060

10 July, 2001

Dear Mr Dennis,

I am most surprised to learn that we have our very own Secret Service! Are you a new outfit? I suppose the point of having a service like this is to keep it secret. Well done, you chaps have done a brilliant job as far as that is concerned. Nor have I ever seen your name in print, which leads me to suspect that "Hilton Dennis" is merely a cunning nom de guerre to limit the possibilities of you being kidnapped and brutally tortured to reveal everything you know about...ah, well, whatever it is you know.

I am in the process of identifying a career path for my boy, Clive. And I feel strongly that the Secret Service would be ideal for him. You will not find a more secretive boy. It took us three years to find out that he had started smoking. And by the time we made the discovery, he had already given up and moved onto stronger stuff. He was always one step ahead of us. In fact, he was wearing skirts long before cross-dressing even became fashionable among the youngsters. To tell you the truth, this is not something of which I am terribly proud. I tried to whip him into shape, but he stole the whip and went round to his Nigerian friends on the corner and exchanged it for a small silver compact filled with talcum powder.

Clive has always shown a keen interest in espionage. In fact, his love of spying has got him into trouble with the neighbours more than once. He is also quick with a Polaroid and knows how to set a fire.

The only problem I can see is that Clive might not meet your demanding physical requirements. He is built more like a schoolgirl than a youth verging on Manhood. Brenda says he will fill out once adolescence is over. But I have my doubts. His hero is an insipid-looking wastrel by the name of Marilyn Manson.

The institute says Clive will be coming home soon. He's got a few more years of school, but it is never too soon to begin identifying a career for your offspring. I plan on being in Pretoria soon, and it might be a good idea if I brought Clive around for an interview.

Unless it is a secret, could you please provide me with your street address?

Yours truly,

....
Ben Trovato (Mr)

SOUTH AFRICAN SECRET SERVICE
REPUBLIC OF SOUTH AFRICA

Private Bag X5, Elarduspark, 0047, Tel: (012) 427 5500, Fax: (012) 427 5970
Delmas Road, Rietvlei, Pretoria

30 September 2001

Dear Mr. Trovato

REF. APPLICATION FOR EMPLOYMENT FOR YOUR SON

Thank you for your letter dated 10 July 2001 in which you request consideration for employing your son in the Service. I wish to apologize for not responding in time.

We have given the necessary consideration to your request and unfortunately, we are not in a position to employ your son.

We appreciate your interest in our Service. Hoping you find a suitable career for your son and wishing you all the best.

Thank you for your understanding.

Yours sincerely

DIRECTOR GENERAL (SASS)
HA DENNIS (MR.)

Mr Ben Trovato
PO Box 1117
Sea Point
8060
Cape Town
South Africa

21 July, 2001

Dear Lord Archer,

How odd to think that you are languishing in a prison cell! You have many supporters in South Africa who are appaled at the manner in which you have been treated. As a teenager I liked nothing better than curling up with A Twist of Sand or A Grue of Ice. In view of what has happened, I suggest your next book be titled A Miscarriage of Justice.

Four years for perjury? Out here in the colonies, we find that sort of sentencing to be completely outrageous. To go to jail for that long, one would have to murder one's mother-in-law and then attack the police when they came to investigate. Even then, one could get away with it by pleading Diminished Responsibility on the grounds that one had been drinking cheap brandy since dawn. Perjury is treated like a littering offence. Most of the time we don't even bother turning up for the sentencing.

So what if you lied about the harlot? That's what men are supposed to do. You can be sure that if Hugh Grant had not been caught with his pants down, he would not have gone around town bragging about his charming encounter with Ms Divine Brown. As far as I can make out, the only difference is that you made a lot of money out of taking the Daily Mirror to court for daring to suggest that you had lain with a woman of ill repute. That took balls, if I may say so. In my experience, fake diaries and false alibis are generally foolproof. Did someone rat you out? Give me his name. I know people who deal with scum like that.

As a one-time deputy chairman of the Conservative Party, I would have expected that Maggie and John Major would have pulled a few strings to get you off. Then again, the Tories are earning something of a reputation as fair weather friends. Do you plan on switching to Labour?

And now they want to strip you of your title? I see a certain Sir Teddy Taylor (Tory) suggests that people like you should be "quietly excluded" from the House of Lords. Should that happen, I suggest you take a leaf out of Sir Guy Fawkes's book.

What is this latest fabrication that you stole millions of pounds destined for Kurdish refugees in Iraq? I see it's another Tory who has the knives out on this one. You managed to raise over 57 million pounds for the Kurds. Now that they've spent it all, they claim to have only received 250-thousand pounds. But it would not surprise me if the authorities took the word of a goat-herding nomad over yours. These are strange times, indeed.

I am enclosing a ten rand note. Tell the thug running the tuck shop that it's worth fifty pounds. When things settle down, let me know if you need anything else.

Yours truly,

Ben Trovato (Mr)

JEFFREY ARCHER

5th October 2001

Strictly Personal & Confidential

Dear Mr Trovato

I must first apologise for the delay in replying to your kind letter to Lord Archer.

Jeffrey has read your letter and wanted to respond personally, but I hope you will understand that he has been overwhelmed with the number of letters he has received, and so has asked me, on this occasion, to reply on his behalf.

The past few months have been, and continue to be, a grueling and unpleasant experience for him and his family, and your willingness to write gives him strength at this difficult time.

Yours sincerely

Alison Prince
Personal Assistant to Jeffrey Archer

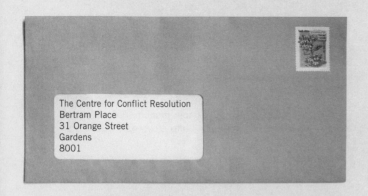

The Centre for Conflict Resolution
Bertram Place
31 Orange Street
Gardens
8001

Mr Ben Trovato
PO Box 1117
Sea Point
8060

22 May, 2002

Dear Sir,

I was pleased to hear that the thirteen "highly-dangerous" Palestinian militants were finally given safe passage out of Bethlehem without any more blood being spilled. That's what I call conflict resolution! Five weeks in any church is enough to break anyone's spirit. More than most, they deserved to begin their exile in sea-facing rooms at the Flamingo Beach Hotel in the resort town of Larnaca on the idyllic island of Cyprus.

I am not one for joining causes, but I am in considerable need of a break. My wife, Brenda, would also appreciate a little time apart. I was hoping you could advise me on the best course of action.

I intend occupying a church (something small, possibly in Bellville) on the second Wednesday in June. Would you suggest that I notify the city council in advance? I would also appreciate any suggestions you may have with regard to selecting a church. Should I go for something high profile, like Roman Catholic, or keep it simple and hole up with the Latter Day Saints? Would a Synagogue be a bad idea?

For this to work, I would need a few armed men to watch the front door. It wouldn't be a proper siege, otherwise. I don't mind if amateur gunmen want to come alone. But they would have to bring their own weapons. Do you have anyone on your membership list who might be interested? I won't be able to pay them, but I will buy lunch.

I am also looking for a negotiator who could get me out before the weekend and into a suite at the Table Bay Hotel by cocktail hour. I am sure you could put me in touch with people who are qualified in this field of work.

I eagerly await your advice and assistance.

Yours truly,

Ben Trovato (Mr)

CENTRE FOR CONFLICT RESOLUTION

Association incorporated
under Section 21

Centre for Conflict Resolution
University of Cape Town
c/o Rhodes Gift Post Office
7707
South Africa
Tel: +27 21 422-2512
Fax: +27 21 422-2622
e-mail: mailbox@ccr.uct.ac.za
http://ccrweb.ccr.uct.ac.za

28 May 2002

2002/15/lm

Dear Mr Trovato

Thank you for your letter of 22 May.

I was sorry to hear that you and Mrs Trovato are in need of a little time apart.

Given the nature of the Centre for Conflict Resolution, and notwithstanding your kind offer of lunch, I'm afraid that I do not have many amateur gunmen at my disposal.

My recommendation regarding a suitable church is that you consider the chapel at Pollsmoor Prison. In the long run this would save you much inconvenience in travel arrangements and would give you access to a large number of amateur gunmen. You are unlikely to get a sea-facing room but the mountain views are excellent and the cocktail hour can be quite merry.

Best wishes

LAURIE NATHAN
Executive Director

Mr Ben Trovato
PO Box 1117
Sea Point
8060

23 May, 2002

The Hon. Kader Asmal
Minister of Education
Private Bag X9034
Cape Town
8001

Dear Minister Asmal,

Congratulations on signing an agreement with Microsoft to provide all 32 000 government schools with free access to Microsoft software. The next generation has to be exposed to technology if this country hopes to produce more Mark Shuttleworths (and more Kader Asmals, for that matter!).

But there is another side to this. An altogether darker, more tragic side. I have a teenage boy, Clive, who spends most of his day staring at a computer screen. I shudder to think what might happen if he were actually allowed to switch it on. His doctor assures me that the day will come when Clive is strong enough tell the difference between fantasies like The Sims and his own, real family.

What I am saying is that computers are dangerously addictive. If one were to use a drug analogy, one could say that the computer is the syringe and the software is the heroin.
Microsoft, like the tobacco companies, is fully aware of this. Microsoft is not a company that gives things away for free. Everything comes with passwords, locks and firewalls.

I understand the agreement will save the government R100 million a year. In the short term, perhaps. But, Minister Asmal, what happens when Microsoft brings out its next upgrade? Will that be free, too? I doubt it. Hundreds of thousands of children will already be hooked on Version XT-6. And when they hear that Version XT-7 is on the market, they will want it. You can bet your life on that. If you think the Soweto riots were bad, see what happens when you tell the kids that there is nothing wrong with the old software. But that's the least of it. Microsoft will have brought out at least two more upgrades by the time the Education Department backs down in a frantic attempt to avert civil war. Once Microsoft is that far ahead, you will never be able to catch up.

This is all part of one man's plan. Children will follow anyone who gives them what they want. Bill Gates is stealing our children. He is stealing children from all over the world. The man has to be stopped before it is too late. He is the Pied Piper of the Cyberworld. Down with Bill Gates! Down with technological imperialism!

I urge you to renege on the agreement.

Yours truly,

....
Ben Trovato (Mr)

MINISTRY OF EDUCATION

Sol Plaatje House
123 Schoeman Street

Private Bag X603
Pretoria 0001, South Africa
Tel.: +27 12 326-0126, Fax +27 12 323-5989

120 Plein Street
Private Bag X9034
Cape Town 8000, South Africa
Tel.: +27 21 465-7350, Fax: +27 21 461-4788

15 July 2002

Dear Mr Trovato

Thank you for your letter of 23 May 2002, and for your interesting views on the Department of Education's recently announced agreement with Microsoft. This is a huge boost to education in our country, and I do not think that I would be serving the interests of our youth by reneging on the Microsoft agreement, as you are urging me to do.

Of course, we believe in moderation in all things. As our Department's Values in Education document clearly states, we shall continue to do our best to encourage our children to find a balance in life, and in this case, a balance between the computer world and the real one. It will be up to individual parents to decide on how much to limit the time their children spend in front of the television or computer screen.

With regard to your concerns about the upgrades, I can hopefully put your mind at ease with the news that Microsoft's generosity in fact extends into perpetuity, with the agreement including the upgrading of donated equipment.

Thank you again for your interest in education, and for sharing your concerns with me.

With my best wishes

Yours sincerely

Professor Kader Asmal, MP
Minister of Education

Dr Ben Ngubane
Minister of Arts, Science and
Technology
Private Bag X9156
Cape Town 8000

Mr Ben Trovato
PO Box 1117
Sea Point
8060

23 May, 2002

Dear Dr Ngubane,

Congratulations on the fine work you are doing. My wife, Brenda, says you are her favourite politician.

I was hoping you might be able to help me with a query. My neighbour, Ted, is planning to hold a fish braai for a group of important overseas visitors in the near future. We were discussing the menu over a couple of beers when he struck upon a brilliant idea. Why not include a coelacanth to go with the snoek and steenbras! It has novelty value and the bigger ones look capable of feeding at least four people.

I seem to remember your ministry announcing that there was a coelacanth run at Sodwana Bay on the North Coast. I hope they haven't been fished out already. I was at St Lucia once and had to fight my way through hordes of blood-crazed rednecks guzzling brandy and gutting fish right there in the shorebreak.

If the fish are still biting, could you advise me on the best bait for coelacanth? Given their history, they are probably smarter than your average kabeljou. You can't really go wrong with fresh squid, but for all I know the coelacanth can't stand the taste of squid. And the last thing I want is to be stuck out at Sodwana with something on the end of my hook that actually repulses the fish.

Any suggestions would be much appreciated. In return, I'll let you know what coelacanth tastes like!

All the best.

Yours truly,

Ben Trovato (Mr)

Mr Ben Trovato
PO Box 1117
Sea Point
8060

29 June, 2002

Dear Dr Ngubane,

I am still waiting for a reply to my letter of 23rd May. I am sure the response has gone astray in the mail, since you have never struck me as a person who deliberately ignores people simply because they happen to be taxpayers.

You may recall that I was inquiring about the possibility of catching one or two coelacanth for a very important braai that my neighbour is planning.

I urgently need to know if they are still biting in the St Lucia area. I would hate to make the trip all the way there only to find that the Boers have taken everything.

I anxiously await your response.

Thank you and keep up the good work.

Yours truly,

Ben Trovato (Mr)

MINISTRY: ARTS, CULTURE, SCIENCE AND TECHNOLOGY
REPUBLIC OF SOUTH AFRICA

Private Bag X727, Pretoria, 0001, Tel: (012) 337 8378 Fax: (012) 324 2687
Private Bag X9156, Cape Town, 8000, Tel: (021) 465 4850/70, Fax: (021) 461 1425

05 July 2002

Ref: AS(0734-2002)

Dear Mr Trovato

POSSIBILITY OF CATCHING ONE OR TWO COELACANTH

On behalf of Dr B S Ngubane, Minister of Arts, Culture, Science and Technology, I acknowledge receipt of your letter dated 29 June 2002.

Minister Ngubane has taken the liberty of referring the matter to his Department for further attention.

Kind regards

MR MABETHA L RALEBIPI
ACT ADMINISTRATIVE SECRETARY

Mr Ben Trovato
PO Box 1117
Sea Point
8060

23 May, 2002

Minister Charles Nqakula
Ministry of Safety and Security
Private Bag X9080
Cape Town
8000

Dear Minister,

Allow me to congratulate you on your appointment to Minister. I hear that crime is already down. Congratulations! You must have some reputation on the streets.

I cannot imagine that you are terribly thrilled with the Constitutional Court's ruling that police may no longer open fire on fleeing suspects. I thought all judges were heavily armed gun freaks. Perhaps that was just in the good old days. Democracy seems to have brought with it a new crop of limp-wristed liberals who believe that it's enough for a policeman to shout "Stop, or I'll...I'll chase you!"

I can't remember when last I saw a policeman running anywhere. There was one moving quickly on foot near my home the other day, but it turned out that he was rushing to get to the bottle store before it closed. Crime fighting now becomes a matter of survival of the fittest. I expect many criminals will be spending their free time in the gym. Perhaps you should consider striking a deal with Virgin Active. Undercover cops could watch the bikes and work out on the treadmill at the same time.

I understand that the ruling also extends to civilians. My neighbour, Ted, has asked me to ask you to clarify something. If someone is running away, and you want to shoot them, would it be alright to run faster than them, overtake them and then turn around and shoot them from the front? In this situation, the target is no longer fleeing. He is running directly towards you, unless he swerves. Did the Constitutional Court say anything about suspects running in a crab-like fashion? What if the suspect is fleeing, but while he is running away he turns quickly and starts to run backwards? What happens then? What about this. A suspect takes off and you give chase, but you are equally fit. Or unfit. You manage to pull up alongside him but can't quite get in front. Is it acceptable then to shoot him in a leg just to slow him down a bit? Or should one simply keep shouting at him in a non-threatening manner until he sees the error of his ways? Ted also wants to know if all else fails, is he legally entitled to throw his weapon at the fleeing suspect's head?

Please could you provide a little clarity before there is a nasty accident.

Best of luck in your new job.

Yours truly,

....
Ben Trovato (Mr)

Mr Ben Trovato
PO Box 1117
Sea Point
8060

29 June, 2002

Dear Mr Nqakula,

I am still waiting for a reply to my letter of 23rd May. I am sure the response has gone astray in the mail, since you do not strike me as a person who deliberately ignores people simply because they happen to be taxpayers.

If you recall, I was requesting clarity on the Constitutional Court's ruling that decent people may no longer open fire on fleeing suspects.

It is absolutely imperative that the position is explained more clearly. There are a few suspects who loiter outside my house every day, and I need to know what my rights are when it comes to opening fire on them.

I hope your reply makes it through the mail this time.

Keep up the good work.

Yours truly,

....
Ben Trovato (Mr)

DEPARTMENT: SAFETY AND SECURITY
REPUBLIC OF SOUTH AFRICA
Private Bag X463, Pretoria, 0001. Tel: (012) 339 2800, Fax: (012) 339 2820
Thibault Arcade, 231 Pretorius Street, Pretoria
tshwete@saps.org.za

4 July 2002

Dear Mr Trovato

RE – FIRING AT FLEEING SUSPECTS

Your letter dated 29 June 2002, regarding the aforesaid refers.

Kindly note that your letter will be brought to the attention of the Minister in due course. You will receive further correspondence in this regard shortly thereafter.

Your patience in this matter is appreciated.

Kind regards.

KRISHNEE KISSOONDUTH
ADMINISTRATIVE SECRETARY (DIRECTOR)

Reference: 3/2/1(55/2001)

**DEPARTMENT: SAFETY AND SECURITY
REPUBLIC OF SOUTH AFRICA**
Private Bag X463, Pretoria, 0001. Tel: (012) 339 2800, Fax: (012) 339 2820
Thibault Arcade, 231 Pretorius Street, Pretoria
tshwete@saps.org.za

Dear Mr Trovato   29 July 2002

RE – FIRING AT FLEEING SUSPECTS

Your letter dated 29 June 2002, regarding the aforesaid refers.

Kindly note that this office has no record of your letter dated 23 May and you would therefore not have received a reply. Further, the Ministry has been informed by the National Commissioner of the South African Police Service as follows:

"It would appear that you are seeking clarity on the Constitutional Court's ruling on Section 49 of the Criminal procedure Act, 1977 (Act No 51 of 1977). The Constitutional Court's ruling is clear and precise and needs no amplification. The Constitutional Court stated (on pages 45 – 46 of the ruling) the following:

(a) The purpose of arrest is to bring before court for trial persons suspected of having committed offences.

(b) Arrest is not the only means of achieving this purpose, nor always the best

(c) Arrest may never be used to punish a suspect.

(d) Where arrest is called for, force may be used only where it is necessary in order to carry out the arrest.

(e) Where force is necessary, only the least degree of force reasonably necessary to carry out the arrest may be used.

(f) In deciding what degree of force is both reasonable and necessary, all the circumstances must be taken into account, including the threat of violence the suspect poses to the arrester or others, and the nature and circumstances of the offence the suspect is suspected of having committed; the force being proportional in all these circumstances.

(g) Shooting a suspect solely in order to carry out an arrest is permitted in very limited circumstances only.

(h) Ordinarily such shooting is not permitted unless the suspect poses a threat of violence to the arrester or others or is suspected on reasonable grounds of having committed a crime involving the infliction or threatened infliction of serious bodily harm and there are not other reasonable means of carrying out the arrest, whether at that time or later.

(i) These limitations in no way detract from the rights of an arrester attempting to carry out an arrest to kill a suspect in self-defence or in defence of any other person."

I trust that this information will address your concerns.

Kind regards.

CHRISTINE MGWENYA
CHIEF OF STAFF

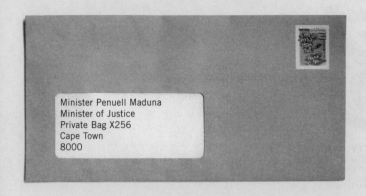

Minister Penuell Maduna
Minister of Justice
Private Bag X256
Cape Town
8000

Mr Ben Trovato
PO Box 1117
Sea Point
8060

23 May, 2002

Dear Minister,

I lead a neighbourhood prayer group and I have been delegated to write to you seeking clarity on your call for Archbishop Desmond Tutu to face charges for questioning the President's judgement in pardoning 33 dangerous criminals. One of the group said he heard you wanted Tutu to return his Nobel Peace Prize, but I think he might have got the facts mixed up.

To be honest, Tutu has never been one of our favourites. He has become far too outspoken since travelling to America. Our democracy is still too young for people to begin speaking their minds. Especially when it comes to questioning decisions taken by the best president we have ever had.

Is there any chance that you could get the Nobel people to take his prize away from him? Telling Mr Mbeki what he should and should not do is certainly not in the best interests of peace and stability. The next thing you know, everyone will want to have a say in how this country is run. What a mess that would be!

Keep doing what you do best – dispensing Justice!

Yours truly,

Ben Trovato (Mr)

MINISTRY: JUSTICE AND CONSTITUTIONAL DEVELOPMENT
REPUBLIC OF SOUTH AFRICA

Private Bag X276, Pretoria, 0001, Tel: (012) 315 1761/2/3 or 315 1332, Fax: (012) 321 1708
Private Bag X256, Cape Town, 8000, Tel: (021) 465 7506/7, Fax: (021) 465 2783

31 May 2002

Dear Mr Trovato

In the absence of Dr Penuell Maduna, Minister for Justice and Constitutional Development, I acknowledge receipt of your letter dated 23 May 2002. The Minister is currently overseas but your letter will be brought to his attention as soon as possible after his return.

With kind regards

J N LABUSCHAGNE
HEAD: MINISTERIAL SERVICES

MINISTRY: JUSTICE AND CONSTITUTIONAL DEVELOPMENT
REPUBLIC OF SOUTH AFRICA

Private Bag X276, Pretoria, 0001, Tel: (012) 315 1761/2/3 or 315 1332, Fax: (012) 321 1708
Private Bag X256, Cape Town, 8000, Tel: (021) 465 7506/7, Fax: (021) 465 2783

26 June 2002

Dear Mr Trovato

In the absence of Dr Penuell Maduna, Minister for Justice and Constitutional Development, I acknowledge receipt of your letter dated 23 May 2002. The Minister is currently overseas but your letter will be brought to his attention as soon as possible after his return.

With kind regards

J N LABUSCHAGNE
HEAD: MINISTERIAL SERVICES

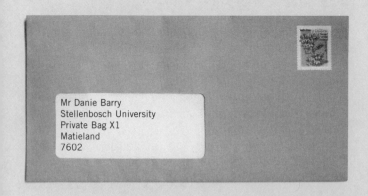

Mr Ben Trovato
PO Box 1117
Sea Point
8060

24 May, 2002

Dear Mr Barry,

I am appaled to hear that the Russians are refusing to return the scientific experiments conducted by our very own Afronaut, Mark Shuttleworth. I understand that the stem cell samples will start to go off in a few days time when the liquid nitrogen begins melting. This is a disaster! Is there anything I can do? I picked up a little Russian while on a trip to Moscow many years ago. A policeman made me put her down. I'm sorry. This is no time for bad jokes. My wife, Brenda, is equally horrified that Mark's entire trip may have been in vain. I asked if she had thought of donating a few of her own stem cells to the university, but the suggestion was not particularly well received.

To be honest, I was never happy about Mark fraternising with the Russians. You may recall the former government telling us over and over that the Russians were not to be trusted. That the Russians were the enemy. They were Communists, for God's sake! We were sent into Angola to fight against these people. Well, not me, but I know of brave men who stood shoulder to shoulder on the 13th parallel and told the Red Devils "Nyet! No further!" Even America warned us that the Ruskies wanted to steal our wives and eat our children. And now they have our stem cells.

I intend writing a very stern letter to the head of the Energia Space Corporation. Russians are cowards, and most of the time they will back down when threatened. The battle of Stalingrad wasn't that long ago. They will know what I am talking about.

Please let me know what else I can do. How about a demonstration outside the Embassy? My neighbour, Ted, is always keen on a protest, especially if it promises to turn violent.

Awaiting your instructions.

Yours truly,

....
Ben Trovato (Mr)

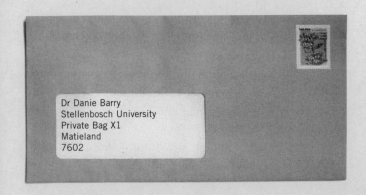

Dr Danie Barry
Stellenbosch University
Private Bag X1
Matieland
7602

Mr Ben Trovato
PO Box 1117
Sea Point
8060

29 June, 2002

Dear Dr Barry,

I am still waiting for a reply to my letter of 24th May. I am sure your response has gone astray in the mail, since you do not strike me as a person who deliberately ignores people simply because they are not academics.

You may recall that I had written to express concern about the fact that the Russians were holding onto the scientific experiments conducted by Mark Shuttleworth during his ride into space.

If the matter remains unresolved, I am still prepared to protest outside the Russian Embassy. Please let me know what the situation is, as I would hate to make a fool of myself.

Yours truly,

Ben Trovato (Mr)

UNIVERSITEIT • STELLENBOSCH • UNIVERSITY
jou kennisvennoot • your knowledge partner

24 July 2002

Dear Mr. Trovato,

RE: ESCD SPACE EXPERIMENT

I refer to your previous letter of 24th of May, which I did not receive. I was away from the end of June until the middle of July to visit students working in Botswana, and have just yesterday receive your letter dated 29 June 2002.

Please rest assured that we have received the embryo and stem cell samples that Mark Shuttleworth returned from the International Space Station. After about four weeks of tough negotiations with Energia, the Russian Rocket and Space Corporation, they agreed to send us the space sample kept stored in a liquid nitrogen tank up to that stage.

We could evaluate our space samples returned to us and compare them to control samples that we have kept on earth in Moscow. We have found significant differences between the space and the control samples in development and structure. This will be reported in a scientific journal shortly.

A appreciate your offer of assistance and loyalty, even to the extent of protesting outside the Russian Embassy.

Yours sincerely,

Dr. DM Barry
Project leader: Embryo and Stem Cell Development Space Program

33

Mr Ben Trovato
PO Box 1117
Sea Point
8060

25 May, 2002

Dear Mr Leach,

I am writing to you with a view to getting my boy, Clive, onto your membership list. I understand that as far as golf clubs go, yours is among the best. Perusing the names of your staff as well as those serving on the committee, I was pleased to see that there no natives among them. I am not a racist, but golf clubs are, by definition, elitist. You do not want to throw membership open to the general hoi polloi. Not unless you want thugs like OJ Simpson strolling the links.

Clive is in his teenage years and has shown a remarkable eye for a ball. He was in line for a position with South Africa's A cricket team, but the institute was unable to sign his release papers in time. I am pleased to report that the lad is now nearing the end of his treatment, and will be looking for something to take his mind off a few nasty incidents that occurred when he was younger. Golf would be perfect.

It might be advisable to let Clive play a few solo rounds before putting him in a foursome. He needs to get back into the swing of things, so to speak. I would not want strangers putting him off his stroke before he is completely ready. I presume you do not allow women to become members? A golf course is no place for the fairer sex. However, I have no objection to them preparing the drinks and snacks at the clubhouse. But it is better for all concerned if they stay off the greens. I am sure you will agree.

Enclosed please find R10 to help Clive to the front of the line. There is more where this comes from. The clubhouse's new Trovato wing is not beyond the realms of possibility!

I look forward to hearing from you soon.

Keep your putter straight!

Yours truly,

....
Ben Trovato (Mr)

ROYAL JOHANNESBURG &
KENSINGTON GOLF CLUB

03 June 2002

Dear Mr. Trovato

We do not know who you are and are not sure whether the tone of your letter is serious or meant to be a joke.

The values of our Club do not coincide with the values expressed in your letter and we therefore regret that we have no interest in pursuing membership at our Club for your son.

Thank you for your enquiry and we return your R10 note.

Sincerely

IAN LEACH
Chief Executive Officer

Mr Ben Trovato
PO Box 1117
Sea Point
8060

5 June, 2002

Dear Sir,

I understand from contacts on the Cape Flats that the Two Oceans Aquarium is looking for certain marine specimens. Well, I am your man. I am in touch with a wide network of informal fishermen who have the entire Atlantic seaboard covered.

I am able to provide you with the finest perlemoen you can ever hope to come across.
Quantity is not a problem. I can easily get you enough for an exhibition tank and more to spare. For ethical reasons I can't say much, but as a marine man yourself, you must already know that the taste of a fresh abalone is almost better than sex. They are not much to look at, I admit. If you want to order a few for one of your tanks, I suggest that you daub the outer shell with streaks of luminous waterproof paint. It makes them look far more exotic. There's not a lot you can do if they choose to suck up against the glass, of course. Should that happen, try to warn tour guides to keep the children away. I have seen married men turn celibate at the sight.

I can get you all the old favourites – lobster, rock cod, red snapper, tuna etc. But I am sure you have more than enough of those on your hands. What about a coelacanth? I am in negotiations with the Ministry of Science and Technology to bag a few. I suggest you get your order in now.

If you need something cheaper, there is always the dusky dolphin. As you know, we have more than we can handle in the Western Cape. Dolphins I can do for five hundred apiece. I prefer to deal in job lots of six. A dozen gets you a complimentary penguin.

Get your order in now before the Spanish pillage the lot!

Yours truly,

Ben Trovato (Mr)

Two Oceans

AQUARIUM

Dock Rd Victoria & Alfred Waterfront

P.O. Box 50603 Waterfront 8002

Cape Town South Africa

Tel (021) 418-3823/4   Fax (021) 418-3952

E-mail aquarium@aquarium.co.za

http://www.aquarium.co.za

12th August 2002

Dear Sir

Thank you for your letter of 5 June 2002. We have our collecting and sourcing of the specimens which we need very satisfactorily in place and are not in a position to take up your offer.

Yours faithfully

p.p. *[signature]*

E.A. FEARNHEAD
Managing Director

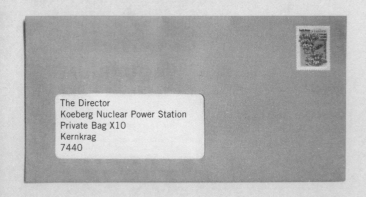

Mr Ben Trovato
PO Box 1117
Sea Point
8060

11 June, 2002

Dear Sir,

I read in the paper that you have put a 26-year-old woman in charge of safety. Dear God, what were you thinking! This is a nuclear reactor we are talking about, not an arts and crafts shop. I am all for equal rights, but the women I know are quite happy to be put in charge of little more than the kitchen.

Women do not even know how to change a plug. Not because they are incompetent, but because their brains are wired differently to ours. Your 26-year-old is no different. Sooner or later, she is going to get confused. Too many flashing lights, gauges and bleeping noises will automatically shut down vital parts of her brain. She only has to press the wrong button and it's goodbye Cape Town.

My neighbour, Ted, says we probably won't even feel a thing. He says it will be like a blast of very hot air and then a millisecond later our flesh and bones will be vapourised. Painless, he assures me. Well, sir, let me tell you that I am far from assured.

What if this woman finds her husband with another man? Do you have any idea what these people are capable of in their quest for revenge? Most of them would not hesitate to destroy an entire city to teach that two-timing bastard the lesson of his life.

Are you prepared to provide me with some sort of guarantee that I will not wake up one morning to find a giant wave of deadly gamma rays heading up my street?

I may have to consider moving my family to somewhere safer, like Durban. At least the Zulus would never put a woman in charge of a nuclear reactor.

Please reconsider the appointment. Tell the woman that it was a clerical error, then fire one of the clerks. If she demands some sort of position, put her in charge of catering.

I anxiously await your words of reassurance.

Yours truly,

Ben Trovato (Mr)

Koeberg Nuclear Power Station

Melkbosstrand, Cape

Private Bag X10
7440 Kernkrag
South Africa
Telephone (021) 550-4911 (Int'l +27 21 550-4911)
Telefax (021) 550-5100 (Int'l +27 21 550-5100)

ESKOM

24 July 2002

Dear Mr. Trovato,

Thank you for your letter and the light relief that you have introduced into my day!

The fact that you have taken the trouble to put pen to paper is commendable in as much as you do appear to have more than a simple passing interest in Koeberg and its relationship with the community it serves. I would personally welcome a visit from you to convince you why you will never have to expect the "blast of hot air"; (and please bring your neighbour, Ted along!) I promise that I won't let any of the women at Koeberg know that you are here, just in case they exercise their "quest for revenge".

Yours sincerely,

PETER PROZESKY
POWER STATION MANAGER

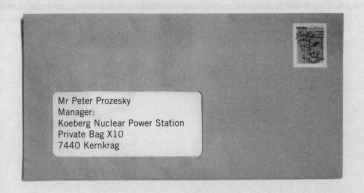

Mr Ben Trovato
PO Box 1117
Sea Point
8060

5 September, 2002

Dear Mr Prozesky,

Thank you for your reply of 24th July to my letter expressing concerns about appointing a slip of a girl to ensure the security of the power station.

I was about to take up your offer of a visit to the facility to set my mind at rest when a band of thugs from Greenpeace beat me to it. But instead of going through the front door like normal people, they chose to go over a five-storey wall surrounding the facility. They even had time to unfurl banners reading "Nukes Out Of Africa" and "Koeberg Sucks".

Where on earth was the girl while all this was going on? Painting her toenails? On the phone to her mother complaining that all men are bastards? She should have been lying belly down in a trench on the beach lobbing mortars at the foreign invaders. Why was she not leading a fixed bayonet charge the moment the marauders set foot on land?

I am horrified that you were unable to prevent your security from being breached by a bunch of limp-wristed, lentil-munching bunny-huggers in little colour-coded rubber boats and lilac jumpsuits. What happens if real men storm the installation? Would you all drop your tea and run shrieking into the suburbs of Melkbosstrand? A fine lot of good that would do.

My wife, Brenda, wants to move to Richards Bay because of this fiasco. I have told her that in the event of an explosion, Knysna would be far enough away. Do you agree?

If you are able to convince Brenda that it is still safe to stay on in Cape Town, my neighbour and I would be prepared to lend Koeberg a hand to keep the vegetarians out. I am a trained Signalman and two semaphore flags are all I need to give the city ample warning of an impending attack. Ted is a sniper. Put him on the roof with his favourite weapon and he could pick off a tourist on Robben Island. Not that he would, of course. All I am saying is that your sea-facing perimeter would be secure.

Brenda has already started to pack. Please let me know urgently if it is safe to stay in the city. And if it is, when do you want Ted and I to report for duty?

Best of luck.

Yours truly,

Ben Trovato (Mr)

 **Eskom**

16 September 2002

Dear Mr Trovato

Once again I must thank you for the interest shown in Koeberg's ongoing business. Particularly , I must thank you for the magnanimous offer of the services of Ted and yourself in the protection of this national asset against the dark forces of evil that would conspire to bring anarchy to the world ! I am truly heartened to know that there are people out there who are unselfishly prepared to step into the breach and to conduct themselves with honour and dignity.

Turning to the recent visit to this establishment by the lilac jump-suit brigade, it is perhaps unfortunate that the media and our eco-terrorists seemed to have missed a fundamental point entirely. This is that Koeberg is actually the most "Green" and "peaceful" form of bulk energy production available in this country! Koeberg is the only energy processing plant in RSA that is completely accountable for ensuring that its waste products will be collected and safely looked after for future generations. In Europe, where 20% of electricity comes from Koeberg's sister plants, there is an avoidance of 20 billion tons of greenhouse gasses per year ! So, our misguided bunny huggers have, as the Afrikaans put it so aptly, "die pot mis gesit!" (and we all know that this leaves a bit of a mess for the rest of us to clean up).

I wish to assure you that your and Ted's services won't be needed just yet. On the day of the "Green invasion", Koeberg's own armed Rambo-brigade was timeously in attendance. When faced with a smiling, young (and not unattractive) New Zealand lassie climbing over the wall, saying "I come in peace", they disappointedly had to find some other use for their itchy trigger fingers! (I'm sure Ted would sympathise). So, there was no real need for our lady operator to begin to break a sweat, let alone to strap on her bandoleers.

You can assure Brenda that her personal health would be far better served by living in Melkbosstrand than in Richardsbay. Remind her of the rather large industrialization in and around that part of the world. I personally would find the choice of domicile a very logical and easy one to make for my family.

Once again, I invite you to come for a cup of tea and a personal tour. Oh, and unless you have a rubber duck and matching jump-suit, and are accompanied by a bevy of suitably attired female attendants, I would recommend you use the front door.

Regards

PETER R. PROZESKY
POWER STATION MANAGER

41

Mr Ben Trovato
PO Box 1117
Sea Point
8060

11 June, 2002

Dear Mr Premier,

I am writing to offer my support at a time when everyone seems to be conspiring against you. It appears that some newspapers have a problem with Mpumalanga taxpayers coughing up R53-million rand for a parliamentary village. Where do they expect your legislators to stay? Among the voters? Hell, no. Politicians have worked long and hard to get where they are today, and they deserve to live apart from the seething masses.

And who are these people demanding that you pay for your own accommodation. This is an outrage! Being a man of the people doesn't mean you have to actually live like them. Here in the Western Cape, our premier gets to live for free in an enormous colonial mansion. But instead of showing their gratitude, our premiers (three in six months) connive with German crooks and rub themselves up against the staff when they think nobody is looking.

I understand that you earn only R600-thousand a year. Converted, this is a mere 40 000 pounds or, if you live in Italy, 139 billion lire. That's barely enough to feed your family, let along pay for your accommodation at the same time.

I have enclosed R10 to help towards the rent.

If you're ever in Cape Town, you are more than welcome to stay with Brenda and I.

Keep up the good work and forget the critics.

Yours truly,

....
Ben Trovato (Mr)

Premier Ndaweni Mahlangu
Mpumalanga Province
Private Bag X11291
Nelspruit
1200

Mr Ben Trovato
PO Box 1117
Sea Point
8060

25 July, 2002

Dear Mr Premier,

I have not yet received a reply to my letter of 11th June. I am sure that it has gone astray in the mail. You do not strike me as a man who ignores people simply because they pay their tax in another province.

If you recall, I was voicing my support for a parliamentary village in Nelspruit. Is it still going ahead? Do not allow the reactionaries to win this battle.

Did you ever receive the ten rand I sent you? There is more where that came from. Just say the word.

I would also like to know if you plan on taking up my offer of a free weekend in our humble home. Brenda is making up the spare room and she needs to know your favourite colour. Something to do with curtains and duvets. I am sure you will agree that, as men, it is best we keep out of this sort of thing. Too much colour coding and the next thing you know you are talking with a lisp and standing about with one hand on your hip.

Let me know as soon as you can about the room.

Yours truly,

....
Ben Trovato (Mr)

MPUMALANGA PROVINCIAL GOVERNMENT

No 7
Government Boulevard
Riverside Park
Extension 2
Nelspruit
1200

Private Bag X 11291
Nelspruit, 1200
Tel: (013) 766 0000
Int: +27 13 766 0000

Office of the Premier

Lihovisi la Ndvunankhulu	I-Ofisi Lika Ndunakulu	Kantoor van die Premier

23 July 2002

File No:P1.40
Enq:Jerry Sikhosana
Tel No:013 7662041

Dear Sir

LETTER OF SUPPORT

1. The above subject refers.

2. The Office of the Premier acknowledge and confirm receipt of your letter dated 11 June 2002 with thanks.

3. By directive from the Premier, the Premier would like to thank you very much for your support and a gift of R10.00

Thank you once more

JK SIKHOSANA
PERSONAL ASSISTANT TO THE PREMIER

44

MPUMALANGA PROVINCIAL GOVERNMENT

No 7
Government Boulevard
Riverside Park
Extension 2
Nelspruit
1200

Private Bag X 11291
Nelspruit, 1200
Tel: (013) 766 0000
Int: +27 13 766 0000

Office of the Premier

Lihovisi la	I-Ofisi Lika	Kantoor van die
Ndvunankhulu	Ndunakulu	Premier

15 August 2002

File No:P1.40
Enq:Jerry Sikhosana
Tel No:013 7662041

Dear Sir

LETTER OF SUPPORT

1. The above subject refers.

2. By directive from the Premier I acknowledge receipt of your letter dated 25 July 2002 and further wish to indicate to you that as matters stand, the Mpumalanga Parliamentary village will be built.

3. Attached find our letter of the 23rd July 2002 which we sent to you.

Thanking you

JK SIKHOSANA
PERSONAL ASSISTANT TO THE PREMIER

Mr Ben Trovato
PO Box 1117
Sea Point
8060

23 June, 2002

The Director
SANCA
PO Box 70389
Durban
4067

Dear Sir,

I read in the paper the other day that a young chap by the name of Castro Chiluba (the son of former Zambian president, Frederick) has been sent to jail for six months for possessing cannabis.

I have a son who is approaching the age where he might well begin experimenting with illegal substances. He has already experimented with pretty much everything else i.e. cross-dressing, arson etc. I would appreciate your expert advice.

The Chiluba boy was arrested at a nightclub with twenty (20) kilograms of cannabis. He appealed for leniency on the grounds that he was merely a consumer, not a trafficker. I am no prude. In fact, I tried the stuff myself when I was younger. Please keep this to yourself. If my wife, Brenda, knew about my past she would have me arrested.

I am trying to find out if 20 kilograms is an average amount for a youngster to take with him when he goes out to the disco on a Friday night. I am asking because I think responsible parents should be able to tell when their offspring are drifting into the twilight world of drug abuse.

If Clive says he's going out and I spot him leaving the house with one of those large, black bin-bags slung over his shoulder, should I worry? What if he says he's going to meet a friend at the pub and comes out of his room wearing his backpack? He may try something more devious, of course. Is it physically possible for a young lad to conceal 20 kilograms of marijuana inside his clothing without it being noticed? I tried it with piles of my neighbour's freshly mown lawn, and I managed to get at least seven kilograms into my brooks and down my shirt before he spotted me and threatened to call the police.

I realise there is a possibility that you may tell me that there is nothing to worry about. That kids are growing up much faster these days. And that 20 kilograms today is like four grams in our time. Maybe this is what it takes for Clive's generation to loosen up and have fun. Please let me know if I should begin strip-searching the boy when he goes out.

Yours truly,

....
Ben Trovato (Mr)

cc. Cape Town Drug Counselling Centre

SANCA
Lulama Treatment Centre
Warman House Adolescent Unit
185 Vause Road, Berea, DURBAN, 4001
Tel: 202-2241, 202-2274 Fax : 201-4643
E-mail : lulama@mweb.co.za

Santa Durban
Alcohol and Drug Centres

SANCA
Prevention Services
Penthouse Out-Patient Clinic
236 - 9th Avenue, Morningside, DURBAN, 4001
Tel: 303-2202 Fax : 303-1938
E-mail : antidrug@mweb.co.za

ALL CORRESPONDENCE TO THE DIRECTOR, SANCA, P.O. BOX 70389, OVERPORT, DURBAN, 4067

03 July 2002

Dear Mr Trovato

Thank you for your letter & your interest in drug abuse. At least, you've maintained your sense of humour, something we really need to do in these challenging times! I will do my best to deal with the various matters you've raised & hope that your concerns will be appropriately addressed.

- I'm glad to hear you're not a prude, & with reference to past indiscretions, you may rest assured that your wife cannot have you arrested in terms of the Drugs & Drugs Trafficking Act (No 140 of 1992). Unless, of course, there's something you're not telling us!!
- If the report on the young man in possession of 20kg of cannabis is true, then the logistics of transporting the stash conjure up images of a Monty Pythonesque nature! What a relief that this is not typical behaviour. Apparently, centuries ago, the nomadic peoples of central Africa made minor tribal law-breakers smoke dagga until they passed out, as a punishment. This led to "green fever", the dagga equivalent of a "babbelas". Imagine what 20kg would do! More seriously, he must have been dealing. Enclosed please find a copy of our booklet on this drug : "Questions & Answers on Dagga" for your reference.
- Strip searching your son as a preventative measure sounds innovative and may be seem tempting when you are faced with a cross-dressing arsonist who shows signs of trying anything once. However, this would most probably have the judges of our constitutional court shaking their august heads in disapproval. Your local branch of SANCA has trained professionals who could guide you in what we term "constructive confrontation", which is a communication strategy for dealing with dysfunction.

I trust this information is helpful. Hopefully by now, your neighbour has calmed down over your creative & informative experiment with his grass cuttings! Thank you for sharing this experience with us.

Yours sincerely

Claire Savage (Mrs)
Senior Information Officer

PS A friend of mine is quite a fan of yours. Thanks for writing! I guess you know only too well, that laughter is the best medicine (drug?)!

THE CAPE TOWN DRUG COUNSELLING CENTRE

03 July 2002

Dear Mr Trovato,

Thank you for your enquiry.
I enclose a booklet which should provide you with some perspective and direction on drug issues.

Regarding your question about 20 kilos of dagga - this is a large amount of dagga, and I presume he would run the risk of being charged with dealing if he was carrying that amount.

Hope you find the information helpful.

Yours faithfully,

Cathy Karassellos
Clinical Psychologist

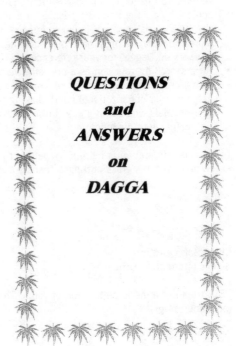

QUESTIONS
and
ANSWERS
on
DAGGA

Mr Ben Trovato
PO Box 1117
Sea Point
8060

22 June, 2002

Ms Cheryllyn Dudley
African Christian Democratic Party
PO Box 2417
Durbanville
7551

Dear Ms Dudley,

I would like to thank you for standing up against that promiscuous group of degenerates who operate under the banner of LoveLife.

As you so rightly point out, our fight is against groups like LoveLife and Planned Parenthood who are anti-family, pro-abortion, pro-licentious sex and deviant lifestyles.It would not surprise me in the slightest if they were communists, too.

I felt very proud to be a South African when you had the courage to stand up in Parliament and enlighten the honourable members as to the true nature of LoveLife's so-called advertising campaign. I had no idea that these whoremongers were openly encouraging our children to pursue such diabolical practices. It borders on Satanism.

I am ashamed to admit that, until fairly recently, I thought the phrase "oral sex" meant talking dirty to your partner. Not that I have ever done this, of course. But these days it's hard to see a film or read a book that does not make reference to such filth. I am appaled that there are groups out there who are publicly encouraging our youth to use their mouths for anything but eating and talking. And this in the name of education!

I was very pleased when Deputy President Jacob Zuma stood up after your speech and said that he felt nauseated. This proved that aversion to oral sex is not a tribal thing. It has nothing to do with being Xhosa or Zulu or even Welsh, for that matter. I have Italian blood and I know for a fact that Sicilian men will not hesitate to kill anyone who suggests that they engage in such a barbaric practice. Even if it is with their own wives.

What do you intend doing about that cross-dressing pervert, Evita Bezuidenhout?

Hope to hear from you soon.

Yours truly,

Ben Trovato (Mr)

PS. Is it true that you were sexually harassed after making your speech in parliament?

49

Mr Ben Trovato
PO Box 1117
Sea Point
8060

20 August, 2002

Dear Ms Dudley,

I have not yet had a reply to my letter dated 22nd June. You have never struck me as being the sort who ignores others simply because they are not Members of Parliament. Your lack of response might not be typically African, but it is not very Christian. On the other hand, it is your Democratic right to decide these things. Your party's name has been well chosen.

On the other hand, your response may well have gone astray in the mail. In which case, I apologise unreservedly.

If you recall, I wanted to know what action you planned to take against those degenerates who run LoveLife and Planned Parenthood. We need to shut them down. And my wife, Brenda, wants to know why the ACDP is so quiet about Pieter-Dirk Uys? The man must be stopped at all costs.

It is not easy for decent God-fearing white people to find a political home these days. The ACDP could be all we have. But if you insist on ignoring us, we may as well be ignored by a powerful party like the ANC.

Brenda and I are looking forward to hearing from you.

Keep up the good work.

Yours truly,

Ben Trovato (Mr)

AFRICAN CHRISTIAN DEMOCRATIC PARTY

Tel. (021) 403 2453
Fax. (021) 461 9690
Email: cdudley@acdp.co.za

P O Box 15
CAPE TOWN
8000

OFFICE OF CHERYLLYN DUDLEY
MEMBER OF PARLIAMENT

16 August 02

Dear Mr Trovato,

Thank you for taking the time to express your concerns and for the encouragement. I have enclosed some press releases and letters which may be of interest to you as they cover some aspects of our continued campaign against PPASA and lovelife campaigns.

Sorry for the delay in responding, as you can imagine we are inundated with so many issues demanding our attention. We appreciate your concern and commitment to truth.

God bless you.

Cheryllyn

Cheryllyn Dudley MP
African Christian Democratic Party

Minister Ngconde Balfour
Minister of Sport
Private Bag X869
Pretoria
0001

Mr Ben Trovato
PO Box 1117
Sea Point
8060

28 June, 2002

Dear Minister Balfour,

Congratulations on taking that old fertiliser farmer, Louis Luyt, to task for his views on the state of rugby which appear in a book co-written by other Afrikaner dissidents. As you so rightly point out, they are nothing but "apartheid dinosaurs" who are trying to "sew mayhem and division" among rugby fans.

I have been a rugby player for most of my life, but was forced to leave the field forever when an old war injury started playing up. But my spirit remains true. And this latest fracas has certainly got the mayhem rising up inside me!

Luyt might have been president of the Rugby Union for fourteen years, but that was at a time when the only black people allowed into Ellis Park Stadium were those bearing trays of beer and biltong.

Luyt has the cheek to issue a statement calling you "uncouth" and "lacking intelligence"! He goes on to say that it's unconstitutional and libelous for you to call him a racist. Then accuses you of racism! The man is clearly confused.

He also says you single-handedly lost South Africa the Olympic Games and the Soccer World Cup. I suppose you are also to blame for the weak rand. And no doubt you had a hand in the plane crash that killed Hansie Cronje. In fact, where were you the day Kennedy was assassinated?

Luyt calls you an "overweight, bloated and big-mouthed minister". That is outrageous. I will bet any money you like that if you both hit the scales, he would turn out to be the whale.

I enclose ten rand towards any libel action you might take against that horrible man.

Yours truly,

Ben Trovato (Mr)

MINISTRY: SPORT AND RECREATION
REPUBLIC OF SOUTH AFRICA
Private Bag X869, Pretoria, 0001, Tel: (012) 334 3100, Fax: (012) 321 8493
Private Bag X9149, Cape Town, 8000, Tel: (021) 465 5506/7/8/9, Fax: (021) 465 4402

12 August 2002

Dear Mr Trovato

Allow me to express my appreciation for the enthusiastic manner in which you support sport and rugby, in particular.

It is quite obvious that you follow South African sport with more than a passing interest and that you are abreast of developments within sport. I found your comments with regard to Dr Louis Luyt very interesting and wish to thank you for the support you have given to me personally.

I have received both your letters but due to the fact that the letter dated 28 June 2002 arrived at a time that my office shifted from Cape Town to Pretoria during the parliamentary recess, I was not in a position to respond immediately. My office attempted to reach you by telephone but this was not possible as you are not listed. In fact, only two companies are listed in the Cape Peninsula telephone directory under the name of "Trovato" and they could not assist me in tracing you.

Nevertheless, thank you for your kind gesture of contributing financially towards what you refer to as "libel action" that I might consider. I have no intention of considering such steps and wish to suggest that you permit me to forward the donation to a project in Cape Town providing sport opportunities for street children.

Your kind-hearted gesture will contribute towards our ideal of providing sport for all in the country. I would love the opportunity to speak to you personally at some time. Could you oblige by calling Graham Abrahams at tel. 021 465-5506 in order for such an arrangement to be made?

I look forward to your response.

Kind regards

BMN BALFOUR
Minister of Sport and Recreation

53

Mr Ben Trovato
PO Box 1117
Sea Point
8060

14 June, 2002

Dear Sir,

I came across your station the other day while attempting to intercept extraterrestrial communications and was momentarily distracted by a catchy little Gershwin tune. All well and good. But suddenly, without warning, you began playing Bach! Dear God, man, do your presenters have such little regard for those of us who fought in the war?

Johann Sebastian Bach was a German. Have you forgotten the lessons learned at Leipzig? Can you ignore the role he played in propping up the despot Prince Leopold of Kothen? And let me assure you, it was no coincidence that Bach was the favourite composer of one A. Hitler. The bloodline ran deep.

I lost many friends to the guns of the cursed Afrika Corps. And I, myself, played no small part in the downfall of Field Marshal Erwin Rommel. You may recall that the death of the man known as the Desert Fox was reported as a suicide. That is about as far from the truth as you can get. But it appears that your station is not interested in the truth. I am old now, but that does not mean you can get away with tormenting us.

I expect an explanation from you, failing which I will have no alternative but to report you to the International War Crimes Tribunal.

Never forget the men of the 21st Division! We died for you. And your family.

Thank you.

Yours truly,

....
Ben Trovato (Mr)

CLASSIC *f*M

102.7

12 August 2002

Dear Mr Trovato

I have not replied to your letter of the 14th of June, due to the fact that I did not receive your communication. Are you sure that you have the correct radio station? – Classic fM has a Gauteng radio license and listeners can only listen to the station on DSTV in Cape Town.

I have noted your concerns about the station playing the music of J.S.Bach. I sympathize that any memories are hurtful. It is however our station policy to continue playing the music of Bach as there is no direct link between Bach and the Nazi era.

Yours faithfully

Mike Ford
Classic fM(SA) Pty Ltd

Mr Ben Trovato
PO Box 1117
Sea Point
8060

14 June, 2002

Dear Sir,

I wish to lodge a complaint about the film, Spider-Man. It is misleading and dangerous. I have always believed that documentaries, by their very nature, are obliged to tell the truth. That they are there to present us with the facts, not lie to us. For that reason, I went along with an open mind, keen to learn something new.

Indeed, I found it fascinating. I was particularly impressed with the cameraman's uncanny ability to be in the right place at the right time. How on earth he noticed the spider dropping down from the roof in the museum is anyone's guess! I imagine he has worked with Sir David Attenborough in the past.

Mr Peter Parker seemed very at ease with having a camera around the whole time. And a good thing too, or we might never have got to witness that incredible transformation.

As a documentary, I found it enlightening (although the music was a little loud in places). And what a coup to finally prove the existence of the Green Goblin! I notice that the sceptics are no longer quite so vocal.

For a week after seeing the film, my neighbour and I collected spiders from the garden. We got at least twenty different kinds into a shoebox. Last Thursday, I waited until Brenda went shopping and then put the box into the microwave oven. I used a low setting so as not to fry the creatures, but just high enough to give them a quick dose of radiation. When I took the box out, most of them were curled up stubbornly refusing to move. But five were hopping about like kangaroos. I quickly poured them down my shirt and waited expectantly. Nothing happened. But later that evening, I noticed a small red mark on my stomach. I went to bed so Brenda wouldn't notice. In the morning, I crept into the bathroom to see my new muscles. However, there was little change. Then I tried squirting high-tensile silk at my sleeping wife. I went through a range of hand movements, but nothing would come out of my wrists. Brenda awoke to find me wiggling my fingers in her face. She reacted badly. And so did I, when I realised that the makers of Spider-Man had perpetrated a deception of monumental proportions.

I urge the Film and Publication Board to either ban this film or have it reclassified from Documentary to Fiction Feature. Please let me know your decision as I may need to take further action.

Yours truly,

Ben Trovato (Mr)

Film and Publication Board

19 June 2002

Dear Mr Trovato

Thank you for your letter of 14 June 2002. I am sorry that you feel betrayed, deceived and misled. The truth, actually, is plainer than the nose on the Green Goblin.

 In the first place, the cameraman happens to be in the right place at the right time because this is a recreation of what actually happened. This is Spidey, better known as the "Webslinger" or "Your Friendly Neighbourhood Spiderman", in flashbacks. We took you back in time, Ben. (How ironic that you should not know this since you share the same name as Spidey's dear old uncle.)

Yes, we managed to expose the Green Goblin. Just in case you missed it. Osborne Enterprises survived and dear old Harry will emerge as the new Green Goblin to avenge his poor old papa's untimely demise.

I am sorry that you failed to duplicate Spidey's powers but maybe you forgot that he got his powers through a spider that was exposed to gamma radiation, not unlike Dr Bruce Banner's alter ego, the Incredible Hulk. Microwave radiation is not gamma radiation. Microwaves involve a range of radio frequencies between about 1GHz to about 300GHz. (To convert from frequency to wavelength, just divide the speed of light 300 000 000 meters per second by the frequency in cycles per second.) You will need a particle accelerator, not a microwave, to produce gamma-rays. (Of course, the Universe is the biggest particle accelerator available but it already belongs to someone else. Unfortunately, the Board, as a secret Government organization, may not loan its own particle accelerator. IN fact, nobody knows if the Board even has a particle accelerator. Its use for the purpose of viewing videos and DVD's for "censorship" was a stroke of genius to hide the fact that it is a particle accelerator.)

I feel I should also warn you about squirting high-tensile silk at wives, whether your's or of others'. In our experience, high-tensile silk has a sophoroforic-aphrodasiaic effect and we have tried to warn people not to use it without protection, especially in view of the need to maintain one-child nuclear families to avoid over-population. Remember, with great power comes great responsibility.

I am also able to confirm that we have reclassified the film as documentary fiction, which is neither documentary nor fiction but truth fictionalized to protect the innocent.

Please remember that Spidey was bitten by an arachnid and not a spider. If you have not already done so, please release all the spiders you have captured.

Your friendly neighbourhood "censor" board.

Iyavar Chetty

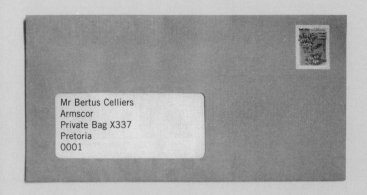

Mr Ben Trovato
PO Box 1117
Sea Point
8060

12 July, 2002

Dear Sir,

I understand that Armscor is selling one of its Daphne Class patrol submarines.

I am very interested in purchasing it. My neighbour and I have already come up with plans to convert it into an aircraft. The shape of the sub makes an ideal fuselage. Ted is very good at metalwork and he has designed a pair of wings to fit the Daphne. Since submarines already have a propeller, we need only replace it with a larger one. We would also need to fit a pair of sturdy wheels to the underside. The controls themselves are very similar. Up, down, left, right. What more do you need?

But anyone can turn a submarine into an aircraft. Our plan is far more sophisticated.

The craft is going to be aeronautically amphibious. It sounds like a highly technical term, but all it means is that our Daphne will be able to operate in both the air and the water. Most aircraft are ill-equipped to fly under water. Considering the number of planes that end up in the sea, this is obviously a major design flaw.

Ted has designed the wings to fold back on themselves. It's the same principle that the Japanese use to make hand-held fans. This means that once the plane is over the ocean, or any large stretch of water, we will be able to retract the wings and go into a steep dive without any fear of death. By the time Daphne penetrates the surface of the water, she will look identical to any other submarine of her class. Except her propeller will be much bigger. Because of this, we estimate that she will be able to travel at speeds of up to 300kph underwater. Using that velocity, Daphne will be able to burst from the ocean and in less than a second the wings will be fully deployed and she will continue flying through the air.

We intend patenting the design, but we are prepared to talk if Armscor is interested in the prototype.

Please let me know as soon as possible if we can pay for the submarine at Simon's Town. Or would you prefer we send a cheque to your office? I have enclosed ten rand as a deposit. There is much more where that came from.

Long live the pioneering spirit!

Yours truly,

....
Ben Trovato (Mr)

CA$H GIVEN R10

58

ARMSCOR

2 August 2002

RE: Daphne Class Patrol Submarines

Sir,

Your letter to Mr Bertus Celliers dated 12 July 2002, refers.

Thank you for your interest. It is with serious concern that we take note of your project plan. Although we find the theory behind the plan sound, we feel compelled to point out the following:
The submarine was designed and built to operate in, and under the sea. This specific design was chosen due to it's exceptional stealth caracteristics whilst submerged. Our concern lies in the fact that the craft might not display the same stealth profile in flight, especially whilst flapping its retractable wings (we assume this forms an integral part of your design). Furthermore, due to its stealth caracteristics, air traffic control might not be able to identify it on radar.

The second concern that we have is with fuel efficiency. Whilst we understand and accept the fact that your design will be super fuel efficient when you dive at a puddle with folded wings, our concern mainly lies with what happens between the time that you burst from the ocean surface until the time you reach the apex of your flight. In this regard, we would suggest pumping vast amounts of Nitrous Oxide (laughing gas) into the "fuselage". It won't make the craft more fuel efficient, but you could potentially have a good laugh at the fuel bill.

All jokes aside, thank you for your letter. It has had its intended effect of entertaining us in our (all too often) serious work environment.

Faithfully

GJ van Staden
Senior Manager
Defence and Industry Support

23 July 2002

REGISTERED MAIL

SALE OF DAPHNE SUBMARINE – SPEAR

Dear Sir,

Thank you for your letter of 12 July 2002, the contents of which have been noted.

Copies of the advertisement published in the Sunday Times and Rapport of 21 July 2002 regarding the sale of the submarine concerned are attached for your information.

Your Ten Rand note (Number: DR 2781179A) included with your letter as a deposit, is also returned since it does not comply with tender conditions.

Yours faithfully

L.P Celliers (Bertus)
Manager: Corporate Communication Division

This Ten Rand note no DR2781179 A issued by the
South African Reserve Bank is the sole property of
Mr Ben Trovato with the indicated postal address of
PO Box 1117, Sea Point, 8060.

Certified as a true version of the situation on this day,
the 22nd of July 2002 at 14:00

L P (Bertus) Celliers
Manager: Corporate Communications
Armscor

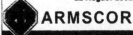
GTO513

Mr Ben Trovato
PO Box 1117
Sea Point
8060

23 June, 2002

Dear Sir,

I have been thinking of emigrating ever since my wife, Brenda, was set upon by two burly men from the local neighbourhood watch. It emerged later that they had mistaken her for a housebreaker. While trying to wrestle free from a lethal stranglehold, she tried telling them that she had a key for the front door. But they laughed and said it's the easiest thing in the world to make copies. She is still wearing a neck brace.

My neighbour, Ted, suggested that instead of emigrating I should get myself a gun. I had my doubts until he told me about your organisation, Free Gun South Africa. He said you provide people with complimentary weapons. I asked him why you would do this, and he said it's because you are good citizens who care about people.

If Ted is telling the truth (for once in his life) would it be possible for you to provide me with more information? I have never owned a gun, so it would be easier for me to choose if you had some sort of catalogue that I could look through.

I have always liked the look of a machine-gun. Ted says I would probably get my picture in the newspaper if I went about wearing a bandolier filled with shiny cartridges. I would also be ready for the armed response people when they launch their next attack.

Even though the gun is free, please accept the enclosed R10 towards postage costs.

Let's go hunting!

Yours truly,

Ben Trovato (Mr)

BRIBE GIVEN
R10

FOR A SAFE AND SECURE NATION

02 July 2002

Dear Mr Trovato

Thank you for your letter dated 23 June 2002. Unfortunately your friend misled you by saying we are giving out guns for free. We are a non-violent organization,

Gun Free South Africa is committed to making a material contribution to building a safe and secure nation, free from fear, by reducing the number of firearms in society. Should you need more information about GFSA visit our website : http://www.gca.org.za

Enclosed is your R10 that you said was donation towards postage costs.

Yours sincerely

....

HB Magubane
Administrator

Mr Ben Trovato
PO Box 1117
Sea Point
8060

13 May, 2002

Dear Mr Marais,

I understand that hordes of women have begun accusing you of sexual harassment. My wife, Brenda, says the allegations cannot possibly be true. She says you strike her as a man singularly lacking in testosterone. As a long-time supporter of yours, I was outraged by her remarks. Unfortunately, by the time I had fetched my stick to teach her a lesson she had already isolated herself in the west wing of the house. I shall deal with her later.

When I heard that all these shrieking harpies were coming forward to report you, there was only one word that went through my mind. Congratulations! There is nothing wrong with men of our age flirting with the office girls. Why should any lass complain of a little slap and tickle on the sly? It's not as if you lured them into the basement with promises of promotion, then ripped their clothes off and had a little congress all of your own. I may be wrong, but I suspect that these vile allegations are being made precisely because you had the decency not to take it further. I have known women who fall into a sex-crazed frenzy simply through a little frottage, whether it be accidental or otherwise.

Be assured that the public think no less of you as a result of these accusations. My neighbour, Ted, has begun regarding you as something of a role model. After a difficult start, most of the ladies in his office now look forward to a bit of a grapple at the photocopy machine. But, as you well know, there are always one or two (or five, in your case) who think their bodies are some kind of Buddhist temple that must remain inviolate. For Pete's sake, even the Church of the Nativity was invaded by Palestinian terrorists! The Taliban actually destroyed giant statues of Buddha! All we want to do is pay a little homage without having to sit through the entire service.

You have worked hard to become the Premier of this fine province. And I am not alone when I say that you, more than most, deserve to indulge in a little recreational activity during the long hours you put in at the office.

You can count on Ted and I for our votes in the next election.

Yours truly,

Ben Trovato (Mr)

PS. Enclosed please find R10 towards your legal cos

Mr Peter Marais
Premier: Western Cape
Private Bag X9043
Cape Town
8000

Mr Ben Trovato
PO Box 1117
Sea Point
8060

13 May, 2002

Dear Mr Marais,

I understand that hordes of women have begun accusing you of sexual harassment. My wife, Brenda, says the allegations cannot possibly be true. She says you strike her as a man singularly lacking in testosterone. As a long-time supporter of yours, I was outraged by her remarks. Unfortunately, by the time I had fetched my stick to teach her a lesson she had already isolated herself in the west wing of the house. I shall deal with her later.

When I heard that all these shrieking harpies were coming forward to report you, there was only one word that went through my mind. Congratulations! There is nothing wrong with men of our age flirting with the office girls. Why should any lass complain of a little slap and tickle on the sly? It's not as if you lured them into the basement with promises of promotion, then ripped their clothes off and had a little congress all of your own. I may be wrong, but I suspect that these vile allegations are being made precisely because you had the decency not to take it further. I have known women who fall into a sex-crazed frenzy simply through a little frottage, whether it be accidental or otherwise.

Be assured that the public think no less of you as a result of these accusations. My neighbour, Ted, has begun regarding you as something of a role model. After a difficult start, most of the ladies in his office now look forward to a bit of a grapple at the photocopy machine. But, as you well know, there are always one or two (or five, in your case) who think their bodies are some kind of Buddhist temple that must remain inviolate. For Pete's sake, even the Church of the Nativity was invaded by Palestinian terrorists! The Taliban actually destroyed giant statues of Buddha! All we want to do is pay a little homage, without having to sit through the entire service.

You have worked hard to become the Premier of this fine province. And I am not alone when I say that you, more than most, deserve to indulge in a little recreational activity during the long hours you put in at the office.

You can count on Ted and I for our votes in the next election.

Yours truly,

Ben Trovato (Mr)

PS. Enclosed please find R10 towards your legal costs.

You certainly have a good sense of Humour. I am returning your R10. You certainly don't deserve your hard earned ☺

Kantoor van die Premier
Office of the Premier
I-ofisi ye Nkulumbuso

30 May 2002

Kantoor van die Premier
Office of the Premier
I-ofisi ye Nkulumbuso

Reference
Verwysing
Isingqinisiso PJM 2002/

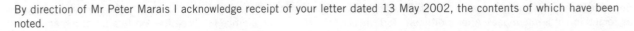

Dear Mr Trovato,

By direction of Mr Peter Marais I acknowledge receipt of your letter dated 13 May 2002, the contents of which have been noted.

Attached find a comment on your letter by the former Premier as well as your R10,00, which cannot be accepted.

Yours faithfully

CI NASSON
ADMINISTRATIVE SECRETARY
Privaatsak X9043, Kaapstad 8000   Private Bag X9043 Cape Town 8000
Tel: +27 21 483 4705/6   Fax: +27 21 483 3421

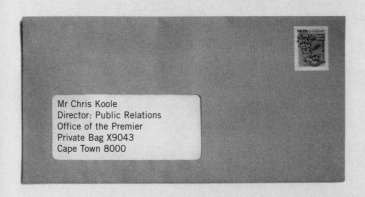

Mr Ben Trovato
PO Box 1117
Sea Point
8060

June 5, 2002

Dear Mr Koole,

You may remember me from a previous correspondence in which I offered Premier Gerald Morkel a selection of alternative reading matter to take his mind off the weighty business of running the province.

Your reply was: "My Premier goes to the Good Book during breaks."

It must have been distressing for you to discover that Mr Morkel was, in fact, going to German fraudster Jurgen Harksen during breaks.

You also said: "My Premier would never judge a fellow man." I could not agree more. Mr Morkel has certainly shown himself to be a man singularly lacking in judgement.

When he was demoted to Mayor, did you go with him? Or are you now serving our new Premier, Peter Marais? Hang on. Hasn't Mr Marais resigned for getting a little too boisterous with the ladies? Gosh, it's hard to keep up.

I understand Mr Morkel has given up his ceremonial duties as mayor. This must leave him with plenty of time. Especially since Harksen is behind bars. Would you suggest I bring a selection of good fiction around to his office?

Hope to hear from you soon.

Yours truly,

Ben Trovato (Mr)

Mr Ben Trovato
PO Box 1117
Sea Point
8060

Chris Koole
Directr: Public Relations
Communication Services
PO BOX 659
8000

7 June 2002

Dear Mr Trovato

I remember our last exchange of letters. I am no longer serving the Premier of the Western Cape and have nothing to do with the Unicity where Mr Morkel, my former boss now serves as Mayor – be it with or without ceremonial functions. This response is in my personal capacity.

With reference to former Premier Morkel and Harksen I find it strange that you have already tried, found guilty and sentenced someone (Mr Morkel) who has not even been heard by the Desai commisson of inquiry. For that matter it seems you have come into the habit of judging and sentencing people before they have been allowed to defend themselves (Mr Marais).

If someone whispered in my ear that you, or whoever, were a former con-artist who had done pensioners out of their lively hood should I just believe it? And if the accuser were a prison inmate or a know crook believing such a story would seem even more far fetched. Accusations remain just that if they are not tried in court. They can then be proven to be defamatory or true. If some-one telephones you a hundred times a day on your cellular 'phone does that mean you were in contact with the caller – even if you did not answer?

Even if Harksen is behind bars he probably still has his cellular 'phone – remember Boesak? You are entitled to your opinion, but let me assure you, and this is from me to you – heart to heart – Mr Morkel is a devout Christian and has set himself high standards. He worked 18 hours a day for this province. If he, like Hansie Cronje, is found to have stumbled along the way – and the funny thing is that all this money talk does not involve personal gain – then he will be judged accordingly. I know Mr Marais well as a former minister and assure you that he too was a hard working man, a good manager and passionate about helping the less fortunate. He too has not yet been tried. And if it comes to pass that he has been too "boisterous", he too will be judged accordingly.

I am still a civil servant employed by the Provincial Administration and true to our code of conduct, steer clear of getting involved in political forays.

Thank you for your letter. I enjoy your humorous (do 'n detect a degree of sarcasm?) style of writing.

Yours truly

Chris Koole (Mr)

Mr Ben Trovato
PO Box 1117
Sea Point
8060

15 June, 2002

Dear Mr Freimond,

I have invented something that will eliminate casualties on South Africa's roads.

In a nutshell, airbags for pedestrians. I call it the Trovato Air-Suit. It works on a similar principle to those found in vehicles. Except the bag is designed to fit the wearer like a wetsuit. Before going for a walk, he slips into his Air-Suit and activates the sensors located in the front and back. These serve to indicate the presence of an oncoming vehicle. The sensor then transmits a signal to the inflating mechanism and within .008 of a second the wearer is surrounded by a protective cushion of air. Since the wearer is now effectively inflated, he will fly some distance depending on the force of the impact. And, much like a beachball, there will be a certain amount of bouncing involved. The important thing is that no physical harm will have been done to the person's body. Since the Air-Suit is worn beneath the clothes, it is unavoidable that the person's outfit will be ruined by the inflating action. However, by simply deflating the Air-Suit, the person can continue going about his day in what resembles a brightly-coloured jumpsuit much like those worn by aerobics instructors.

My invention will make me a millionaire many times over. And the last thing I want is some crook stealing my idea.

Is the Trovato Air-Suit now patented, or is there something else I have to do?

Please let me know soon.

Yours truly,

Ben Trovato

Mr Ben Trovato
PO Box 1117
Sea Point
8060

20 August, 2002

Dear Sir,

I wrote to a Mr Ian Freimond at Patent Services on the 15th of June. Since I have not yet received a reply, I assume that Mr Freimond has either moved on or you have a policy of ignoring ordinary taxpayers wishing to patent a new device.

I was enquiring about the possibility of patenting the Trovato Air-Suit™, which is essentially airbags for pedestrians.

I hope your silence is not an indication that you are planning to steal my idea.

If I do not hear from you by the end of the month, you will leave me with no alternative but to notify President Thabo Mbeki who is personally spearheading the moral regeneration of this great country.

Thank you.

Yours truly,

Ben Trovato

McCALLUM RADEMEYER & FREIMOND
Intellectual Property Law: Patents and Trade Marks

Physical Address:
Maclyn House, 7 June Avenue,
Randburg, Johannesburg

Telephone (011) 789-1046 Telefax (011) 787-4516 Docex 5 Randburg
e-mail: mcrafr@iafrica.com

Postal Address:
Box 1130, Randburg,
2125, South Africa

28 August 2002

Our Ref: MISC/T/IF

Dear Sir,

Re:NEW PATENT APPLICATION

We refer to your letter dated 20 August 2002 addressed to Mr. Ian Freimond from our office. Mr. Freimond is currently abroad and will attend to your letter upon his return in the second week of September 2002.

We can not find any record of the letter of 15 June 2002 you refer to. You are welcome to contact the writer hereof at the above-mentioned telephone number should you desire any further information.

Yours faithfully,

McCALLUM, RADEMEYER & FREIMOND
Per: Danie Dohmen

Mr Ben Trovato
PO Box 1117
Sea Point
8060

20 June, 2002

Dear Mr Gaum,

I would like to congratulate you on your decision not to allow condoms to be distributed to schools in the province.

You are absolutely right when you say that this would condone sex among adolescents. If the liberals had their way, the school corridors would be awash in copulating teenagers. Detention would become an opportunity for group sex among grade twelves and, at the very least, heavy petting among the lower standards.

Installing condom dispensers in the restrooms does not encourage abstinence. It encourages the filthy-minded little bastards to experiment. And anyone who has ever studied science or biology will know that experiments lead to accidents. Accidents along the lines of: "Oops! My lunch money accidentally fell into the slot marked Rough Riders." Then young Susie accidentally forgets to wear her knickers to school. The next thing you know, there are babies everywhere.

And the critics dare to call you irresponsible!

My wife, Brenda, says that with your aversion to condoms you must be Catholic. I disagreed strongly and chased her out into the garden. I say that you are acting in the best interests of our children. I would appreciate it if you could settle this argument for us.

Looking forward to your reply.

Yours truly,

Ben Trovato (Mr)

Telefoon
Telephone   (021) 467-2523
IFoni

Faks
Fax   (021) 461-3140
IFeksi

Verwysing
Reference   20020607-0014
ISalathiso   3/1/9

Ministerie van Onderwys

Ministry of Education

I-Ofisi yoMphathiswa wezeMfundo

28 June 2002

Dear Mr Trovato

NON-DISTRIBUTION OF CONDOMS IN SCHOOLS

On behalf of Adv. A Gaum, Minister of Education: Western Cape, I acknowledge with thanks receipt of your letter dated 20 June 2002, the contents of which have been noted.

You could be expecting a reply in due course.

Kind regards,

EDDIE KIRSTEN
HEAD: MINISTRY
DATE: 28-6-2002

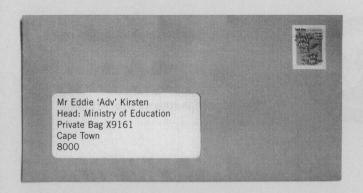

Mr Ben Trovato
PO Box 1117
Sea Point
8060

25 July, 2002

Dear 'Eddie',

Thank you so much for your considered reply to my letter of 20th June.

I was most pleased to hear that your department remains steadfast in its refusal to supply free birth control devices to schools in the province. As you so rightly point out, the last thing we want to do is send out a message that promiscuous sex on a massive scale is acceptable. You are probably old enough to remember what happened in America in the 1960s when guilt-free sex became fashionable (even though none of us were able to be there because of discriminatory visa policies that were enforced as a result of our own policies of perceived discrimination). I need not bring your attention to the multitude of corporate scandals that are currently rocking the global money boat. The papers are full of the filthy details. And where did these crooked CEOs come from? I will tell you. They are the spawn of the summer of love. But as an educated man, you know this already. All I ask is that you watch out for the Americans. They are not what they seem to be. They could not possibly be.

Eddie, I am reluctant to unmask you. But we live in times that demand total honesty. As a senior politician, you will appreciate this. Maybe not now, but some day you will thank me. During our correspondence it has become clear to me that 'Adv Gaum' does not exist, even though you say you speak for him. At first, I was deeply conflicted. I felt betrayed and began drinking heavily. It was only this morning that I realised I was being too hard on myself. I think you have chosen a fine pseudonym. It carries with it a whisper of the indigenous folk of Africa and yet something of the South Pacific at the same time. I found this realisation comforting enough to allow me to sleep soundly for the first time in days. But last night I awoke with terrible thoughts coursing through my mind. What if there really is an Adv Gaum and he is using 'Eddie Kirsten' as his nom de guerre?

You may be relieved to know that I allowed Brenda back into the house to help resolve this conundrum. Unfortunately she made straight for the refrigerator and it was five hours before she stopped eating long enough to make sense. All the while, I was chattering away about abstinence and monogamy, but when I tried to explain my theories about Gaums and Eddies her eyes rolled back in her head and she fled for the garden with her mouth and hands full of soggy vegetables and bruised fruit.

Well, Mr Eddie Adv Kirsten Gaum. Best of luck. Regards to the 'wife'.

Yours truly,

Ben Trovato (Mr)

Telefoon
Telephone (021) 467-2523
IFoni

Faks
Fax (021) 461-3140
IFeksi

Verwysing 20020607-0014
Reference 3/1/9
ISalathiso

Ministerie van Onderwys

Ministry of Education

I-Ofisi yoMphathiswa wezeMfundo

22 July 2002

Dear Mr Trovato

NON-DISTRIBUTION OF CONDOMS IN SCHOOLS

Further to my acknowledgement of your letter of 20 June 2002, I have the priviledge to once again correspond with you on behalf of the Western Cape Minister of Education. I must also remind you that we have previously corresponded on another matter to which I received public acknowledgement.

Thank you for your clear support to the comment by Minister André Gaum. You obviously support the idea that we are not going to distribute condoms at schools because we do not want to create the impression that sexual activity is part and parcel of everyday school life. We do not want to create the impression that this is acceptable and that it is seen simply as an issue that should be managed.

The Western Cape is rolling out a massive HIV/AIDS programme in primary schools and high schools, as Adv. Gaum already indicated. We do agree that condoms should be more freely available, for example, at medical clinics and other venues, at all hours. Our peer educators in high schools will be able to advise learners on where they can obtain condoms, should they wish to obtain them.

Our information is that learners are already collecting condoms at medical clinics, where the Department of Health is making it available. We will liaise further with the department to consider ways in which to make condoms more freely available. This will however not include making them more available on school premises.

Meanwhile, our message will continue to be "ABC" – Abstinence, Be faithful, and if you can't do either of these, then use a Condom. We are indeed teaching this to learners in our schools. As you so clearly argue, an added problem is that teenagers like to experiment. If we start handing out condoms in schools on a massive scale, our efforts may be counterproductive.

Like yourself, we also support the call of the President for moral regeneration in the country. Part of the message must say that promiscuous sex on a massive scale is unacceptable, and you do not necessarily need to be Catholic to support this.

Kind regards

EDDIE KIRSTEN
HEAD: MINISTRY

PS: Regards to the wife, sorry that she lost the bet and please let her back in from the garden, it is freezing out there.

Mr Ben Trovato
PO Box 1117
Sea Point
8060

Mr Eddie Kirsten
Private Bag X9161
Cape Town
8000

13 August 2002

Dear Ben (If I may be so familiar)

I can appreciate your confusion and frustration. It is quite common for such anxiety to lead to conspiracy theories. I am however very pleased to confirm that Eddie actually exists as a separate, mostly independent person who is remunerated thanks to your kind contributions to the state coffers through SARS. I am a humble servant to the people and slave to the cause. Not elected but appointed I have been running offices for ministers for many years. I have lived through the total onslaught, experienced the liberation and thus far, even survived the politics of the Cape of Storms. I have seen many different things and a lot of the same thing. A politician, I will never be, you must be born that way.

My response to you is cautious as it should be. I am not a learned man like yourself so 'Adv.' is not for me and even though I am a humble servant, I am nobody's nom de guerre.

Although I would love to, I will refrain from commenting on the topics of bruised fruit, abstinence and monogamy. Being a WAM, I had to consult a dictionary to find out what these words meant and in conclusion I decided that they were indeed foreign words to this continent.

I trust that now this matter is cleared up, your sleeping patterns will improve and Brenda will be saved from seeking comfort in the garden all the time.

Please convey my kindest regards to the 'wife'.

Yours sincerely

EDDIE KIRSTEN

Mr Ben Trovato
PO Box 1117
Sea Point
8060

20 June, 2002

Minister Dullah Omar
Minister of Transport
Private Bag X9129
Cape Town
8000

Dear Mr Omar,

Each year, 9 000 pedestrians and cyclists are killed in Europe. In traffic accidents, I mean. If you include ethnic cleansing and terrorist attacks, the number would be considerably higher.

I need not tell you that we have a similar problem in South Africa. It is even more serious here than in Europe. Our drivers actually swerve towards pedestrians. I once saw a car mount the pavement in Adderley Street and chase a group of people a hundred yards down the road. You may have heard of a recent case in Cape Town where a motorist stopped his car, got out a baseball bat and proceeded to assault a cyclist. Another motorist simply sideswiped an entire pack of athletes training for the Argus Cycle Tour.

I have invented something that will reduce, if not eliminate, the number of casualties on the roads. In a nutshell, airbags for pedestrians. I call it an Air-Suit. It works on a similar principle to those found in vehicles. Except the bag is designed to fit the wearer like a wetsuit. Before going for a walk, he slips into his Air-Suit and activates the sensors in the front and back. These serve to indicate the presence of an oncoming vehicle. The sensor then transmits a signal to the inflating mechanism and within .008 of a second the wearer is surrounded by a protective cushion of air. Since the wearer is now effectively inflated, he will fly some distance depending on the force of the impact. And, much like a beachball, there will be a certain amount of bouncing involved. The important thing is that no physical harm will have been done to the person's body. Since the Air-Suit is worn beneath the clothes, it is unavoidable that the day's outfit will be fairly ruined by the inflating action. However, by simply deflating the airbag, the person can continue going about his day in what resembles a brightly-coloured jumpsuit much like those worn by aerobics instructors.

I am in touch with the people at Patent Services. Production of the Trovato Air-Suit is likely to begin in early summer.

I need to know how many Air-Suits your department will be ordering.

Let's keep death off the pavements!

Yours truly,

Ben Trovato (Mr)

77

MINISTRY: TRANSPORT
REPUBLIC OF SOUTH AFRICA

Private Bag X193, Pretoria, 0001, Tel: (012) 309 3131, Fax: (012) 328 3194
Private Bag X9129, Cape Town, 8000, Tel: (021) 465 7260/4, Fax: (021) 461 6845

2 July 2002

Dear Mr Trovato,

re:AIR SUIT

I am writing to you in connection with the letter you wrote to Minister Omar regarding the matter highlighted above.

The National Department Of Transport will not be purchasing any of the air suits you have manufactured. Thank you for the offer.

Kind Regards,

NOMSA MAEKO
ADMINISTRATIVE SECRETARY

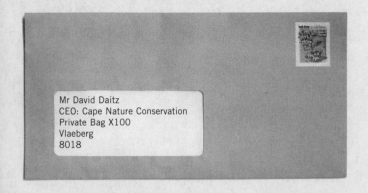

Mr David Daitz
CEO: Cape Nature Conservation
Private Bag X100
Vlaeberg
8018

Mr Ben Trovato
PO Box 1117
Sea Point
8060

28 June, 2002

Dear Mr Daitz,

I would like to voice my support for Cape Nature Conservation's decision to establish a 4x4 trail through the Cedarberg Wilderness Area. It's a wonderful idea and I can hardly imagine why you never thought of it sooner.

I own a small bakkie and have often wanted to take it off the road to see what it is really capable of doing. It's actually a 2x4, but with the difflock on you can hardly tell the difference. In fact, I tried it once when I took my wife to see the flowers in the West Coast National Park. That was in the days when we were still talking to one another. It ended badly when we got stuck in a field of Namaqualand daisies and Brenda had to push us out. Then a posse of fascists in khaki uniforms turned up and threatened to shoot us if we left the road again. I had to fall back on my military training, but even so, it was a day I would rather forget.

I have told Brenda that we can now take Le Big Blur (the bakkie's name) on a legitimate off-road adventure. But when I came to look for the keys they were gone. She denied everything (don't all women?) and I have had to pay for a man to come out and tow the car away so they can dismantle the lock and make a duplicate key.

I have been to the Cedarberg only once, but I clearly remember coming across many trails that could comfortably accommodate seven hikers walking abreast of one another. As a man of nature yourself, I need not tell you that hikers prefer to walk in single file. They do not march down the trail like a platoon of jackbooted storm troopers. The average 4x4 is no wider than four hikers standing shoulder to shoulder. This means there is plenty of room for the walkers to squeeze past. The only problem I foresee is hitchhikers clogging up the pedestrian arteries once they see how quickly we can reach the Bushman paintings. We move freely with cases of ice cold beer. The average hiker carries a litre of luke warm water. The purists will be won over in no time at all.

I understand there is some ponce by the name of Bill Bainbridge who says that "it is clear that the notion of a four-by-four trail within a wilderness area does not accord to either local or international guidelines". I mentioned this to my neighbour, Ted Goodfellow. He seemed to feel that Mr Bainbridge needed to get laid. In the back of a bakkie, preferably.

Our Mr Bainbridge says it is unethical for state agencies like Cape Nature Conservation to engage in self-funding activities. He says the "public purse" has to bear the costs of managing protected areas for the greater good. I shall be having a word with the Receiver of Revenue to ascertain that Mr Bainbridge is declaring his purse adequately.To quote Mr Bainbridge once again: " public access by vehicle into wilderness areas was never permitted in the past." Have you considered reminding Mr Bainbridge that public access by black people into public toilets, parks, beaches, cinemas and shopping malls was never permitted in the past?

Two years ago, the very same Mr Bainbridge said the Cederberg was "absolutely safe in the hands of Cape Nature Conservation". What happened to him between then and now? Did you take him off the payroll? Did his wife hide his medication? Is he related to Ted Kaczynski, the well-known Luddite who is serving three life terms in an American jail?

Please accept this ten rand note towards your fight to open up the trails for those of us who think walking is an abomination.

Yours truly,

....
Ben Trovato (Mr)

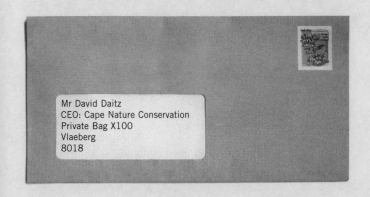

Mr Ben Trovato
PO Box 1117
Sea Point
8060

4 August, 2002

Dear Mr Daitz,

You have not yet replied to my letter of 28th June. I have heard that you are a man who takes his responsibilities seriously, so I assume your reply has gone astray in the mail.

If you recall, I sent you ten rand towards your campaign to establish a 4x4 trail through the Cedarberg Wilderness Area.

Since there was so much opposition to the idea, I assumed you might have to go to court to get your way. In which case, you will need more money.

However, I am reluctant to send more cash since the previous donation has gone unacknowledged. For all I know, your secretary slipped it into her purse to buy nail polish or drugs. Or something.

Please let me know if you got the money and if this is a safe address to continue sending donations in support of the cause.

Keep up the good work and let's get those trails open!.

Yours truly,

Ben Trovato (Mr)

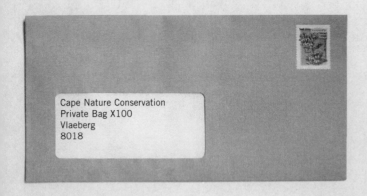

Cape Nature Conservation
Private Bag X100
Vlaeberg
8018

Mr Ben Trovato
PO Box 1117
Sea Point
8060

23 August, 2002

Dear Sir,

I have received no response to previous letters addressed to Mr David Daitz on the 28th of June and the 4th of August. I was under the impression that Mr Daitz was in charge of Cape Nature Conservation. However, it now appears that he goes under another name when receiving mail from the public.

I have given 'Daitz' money towards his campaign to open up the Cedarberg Wilderness Area to 4x4 vehicles. Since I have not heard from him, I assume his campaign has succeeded.

I am in the process of getting together a group of friends for an off-road bash through the park sometime next month. There will probably be around twenty vehicles. Some of the chaps are quite adventurous so it is unlikely that we will be sticking to any marked trails.

Tell 'Daitz' that he is welcome to join us.

Yours truly,

....
Ben Trovato (Mr)

**Western Cape
Nature Conservation Board**

Private Bag X100, Vlaeberg, 8018
106 Adderley Street, CAPE TOWN 8001
Website: www.capenature.org.za

**Wes-Kaapse
Natuurbewaringsraad**

Privaatsak X100, Vlaeberg 8018
Adderleystraat 106, KAAPSTAD 8001
Webadres: www.capenature.org.za

6 September 2002

Dear Mr Trovato,

I have offended you quite clearly although this was not my intention. Water under the bridge cannot be regained so I can do no more than offer my sincere apologies and an explanation, which I appreciate, is not adequate but I can do no more.

I did receive both your letters, of 28th June and 4th August. I enjoyed the humour of the first letter. My sense was that the R10-00 note attached was intended to reinforce the humour. While it is true that every cent can be made to count, we are not in the business of accumulating large numbers of small donations in order to provide significant resources to achieve a particular objective. Belatedly, thank you for your donation, which was clearly given with serious intent although I didn't appreciate that at the time.

I received your letter of 4th August in the midst of hectic preparations for my involvement in WSSD amongst other things. I tried to find a telephone number so that I could call you but if you do have a landline, it appears to be unlisted. A suitable answer to you was on my list of things to do before I left for WSSD but it was, I regret to say, one of a number of things I did not get to. Once again, I hope that you will see your way clear to accept my apologies.

To address the substance of the matter, neither I, nor the Western Cape Nature Conservation Board is on a campaign to open the Cederberg Wilderness Area to 4x4 vehicles, but we are interested in trying to achieve agreement between various user groups regarding the use, on a controlled basis during limited windows of time, of the Pakhuis Pass to Heuningvlei road. So I regret to advise, in the event that the assumption of paragraph 2 (letter dated 23rd August) is serious, that the attempt to achieve consensus is on-going but as yet, unsuccessful.

Thank you for the invitation to join you for your 4x4 off-road bash but these activities have never appealed to me personally, so I will decline.

I trust that the park you will be bashing through both on- and off-road is private property because such activities have no place within the Cederberg Wilderness Area.

Yours sincerely

DAVID DAITZ
CHIEF EXECUTIVE OFFICER

Mr Ben Trovato
PO Box 1117
Sea Point
8060

30 June, 2002

Dear Sir,

I was watching the telly the other night when a SASOL advertisement came on. I almost fell out of my chair, such was my dismay.

The advert featured a multi-racial group of children. But this is not what horrified me. Let me tell you that I very nearly choked on my cognac when I heard the song that was being played. You know what I am talking about. It is beyond comprehension that you could choose a song by that communist band, The Beatles.

As if that is not bad enough, you go one step further and select something sung by that drug-addled bisexual hippy John Lennon. In case you have forgotten, let me recite the chorus for you: *"I get high with a little help from my friends."*

Dear God, man, what were you people thinking? This is an advertisement for a company that produces petroleum products. What message are you sending out? Are you deliberately encouraging our children to spend their time at the corner garage sniffing petrol fumes when they could rather be in self-defence classes learning how to stay alive in today's violent and promiscuous society?

Are you in competition with the glue companies?

I used to mix with a crowd of petrol-sniffers when I was young and foolish, and I have seen what this stuff can do to an undeveloped mind. I will never forget Bennie van der Ploeg, a bright kid who used to get top marks until he started hanging around the local Shell pretending to pump up his bicycle tyres and ending up slumped semi-conscious from inhaling long and hard at the pumps. Bennie is a vegetable today.

You simply cannot tell the younger generation that they have friends at SASOL who will help them get high.

Please let me know what you intend doing to remedy the situation. I will not hesitate to lead a boycott of all SASOL products. If you have to have music in your advertisements, I suggest you use a wholesome band. Stay away from sluts like Britney Spears and that other dusky one with the devil in her eyes. A little Sinatra would not hurt anyone.

I look forward to hearing from you soon.

Yours truly,

Ben Trovato (Mr)

Mr Ben Trovato
PO Box 1117
Sea Point
8060

4 August, 2002

Dear Sir,

I have not yet received a reply to my letter of 30th June. I am sure it has gone astray in the mail, since you must surely be aware of the potential consequences of ignoring members of the public who make regular use of Sasol products but who are quite capable of switching to another company's products without any qualms whatsoever.

You may recall that I expressed my concern about Sasol's latest television advertisement which features a Beatles song calling on people to get high with a little help from their friends. Making matters worse, the advert features young children who hardly need encouragement to take mind-altering drugs.

Should I not hear from you in this matter, you will leave me no choice but to approach the Advertising Standards Authority, the Broadcasting Complaints Commission and my neighbour, Ted Goodfellow, who is a veteran of consumer boycotts.

Thank you.

Yours truly,

....
Ben Trovato (Mr)

sasol
reaching new frontiers

19 August 2002

Dear Mr Trovato

Thank you for your letter of 4 August 2002. Brenda Kali, Sasol's Manager Group Communications and Public Affairs, responded to your 30 June 2002 letter on 11 July, 2002.

I have noted your concerns along with the numerous positive responses received by Sasol regarding Sasol's latest television and other media advertisements.

Yours sincerely

P V COX

Mr Ben Trovato
PO Box 1117
Sea Point
8060

24 August, 2002

Dear Ms Kali,

You may remember my letters of 30th June and 4th August in which I expressed concern about your latest advertising campaign. However, it is possible that you may not remember sending your "reply" to me.

I have since heard from your boss, Mr Cox, who tells me that you responded to my letter on the 30th of June.

Ms Kali, we both know that you never wrote that letter. The entire affair reeks of a cover-up that goes all the way to the top. Would you be prepared to take a polygraph test stating that you did, in fact, reply to my letter? And that you actually posted said reply? The mail service is extremely efficient in this country. I can testify to that. Perhaps it slipped to the bottom of your handbag. Have you checked?

All I want is your response to my complaint. I am not even complaining about the amount of benzene, vinyl chloride and methylene chloride that you put in your petrol. Nor do I particularly care that the good folk of Sasolburg are inhaling air mixed with nearly one hundred thousand tons of hydrogen sulphide, hydrogen dioxide and a whole bunch of volatile organic compounds. So long as our children are not encouraged to get high with a little help from their friends.

I am sure you have kept a duplicate of your "response" to my concerns. I suggest you make a copy, pop it into an envelope, slap a stamp on it, make sure my address is on it and slip it into a mail box. The post office insists that these steps be followed for them to do their job properly.

Let's hear from you this time.

Yours truly,

....
Ben Trovato (Mr)

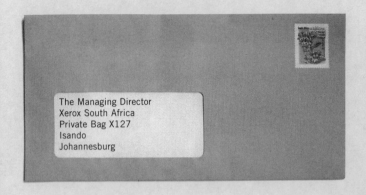

Mr Ben Trovato
PO Box 1117
Sea Point
8060

30 June, 2002

The Managing Director
Xerox South Africa
Private Bag X127
Isando
Johannesburg

Dear Sir,

I was on the point of buying shares in your company when I opened my newspaper this morning and discovered that Xerox shares had fallen by 15 percent. To be honest, I was shaken. I could not imagine what kind of global disaster might have sparked such a panic. After all, your company makes photocopiers.

Then I discovered that the share price had plummeted because Xerox "confessed" that it had "overstated" its revenue by 1.3 billion pounds in the past five years. What a damn fool thing to do! This isn't the Catholic Church. Why go around confessing these things? I thought you people were trained not to crack under pressure. Every company has a little bit of how's-your-auntie going on in the accounts department. Admittedly, not everyone moves their decimal point 16 billion rand to the left. But if your chaps don't have a head for heights they shouldn't be doing the rigging.

I'm not suggesting this happened at the Johannesburg branch, of course. Finger-trouble on this scale only happens at head office, which is invariably located in Washington or New York. This is even more worrying, because the Thief-in-Chief, George W Bush himself, was quoted as being "mad as hell" at the pillaging that is now taking place in corporate America. And we all know what happens when the "President" gets upset. He takes it out on us and Argentina. So now I must pay more for petrol and cognac because some Harvard-educated pimp in a suit snapped when the heat was on.

Is it possible that the number crunchers have made an innocent mistake? After all, any drug-soaked accountant working for a company that exists purely on the principle of duplication might well find himself subconsciously replicating the end of year figures.

Can you assure me that you have not contributed to this fine state of affairs? Would you suggest that I invest my money in a company that is unlikely to be targeted by smart bombs in any future US-led campaign against inaccurate bookkeeping?

I have money. Let me know what you think I should do with it.

Yours truly,

....
Ben Trovato (Mr)

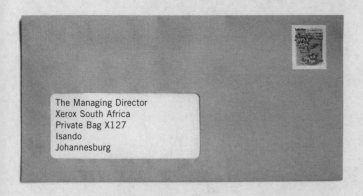

Mr Ben Trovato
PO Box 1117
Sea Point
8060

4 August, 2002

Dear Sir,

I have not yet received your reply to my letter of 30th June.

If you recall, I was seeking assurances that it is safe to invest in Xerox after it emerged that the accountant at head office had got his figures wrong by R20-billion or so.

Under the circumstances, would you suggest holding back on the purchase of shares at this point in time? I appreciate that you are a businessman and not a financial broker, but if it turns out that your company has more in the petty cash box than it does in the bank, I might want to take my money somewhere else.

Any thoughts on the matter?

Yours truly,

Ben Trovato (Mr)

THE DOCUMENT COMPANY
XEROX.

8 August 2002

Dear Mr Trovato,

I am in receipt of both your letters and would appreciate it if you would call me at the office so that we may discuss the contents thereof.

My number at the office is (011) 928-9100.

I look forward to hearing from you.

Yours sincerely,

ROB ABRAHAM
MANAGING DIRECTOR

Mr Ben Trovato
PO Box 1117
Sea Point
8060

3 July, 2002

Department of Transport
Private Bag X193
Pretoria
0001

Dear Sir,

I am a regular user of the train service in Cape Town, but increasingly I find myself opting for the bus. It is not the trains that are the problem. In fact, with all the missing windows I find the ride rather refreshing. It's the other passengers that are beginning to disturb me. The women, actually.

Put more than three of them together, and by the time you reach your stop the casual chatter has reached a deafening crescendo of screeching and yelling. It's not unusual to have up to a dozen females in the same coach, and I frequently have to alight from the train several stops early to avoid permanent damage to my eardrums.

This is why I am so pleased to hear that Education Minister Kader Asmal has called on Transport Minister, Dullah Omar, to consider restricting some carriages for the use of women passengers only. Mr Asmal has clearly had experience of travelling in a confined space with members of the louder sex.

Please advise Mr Omar that the decibel levels in women-only coaches are likely to cause physical harm to anyone even standing on the platform. I suggest that these special carriages be soundproofed to avoid potential lawsuits. I have some experience in this field (I had my study insulated to drown out my wife's voice). Please let me know if the minister would like me to share my ideas on this. I can visit him in Pretoria, if need be.

Looking forward to hearing from you.

Yours truly,

Ben Trovato (Mr)

Ministerie van Gesondheid

Ministry of Health

Umphathiswa weZempilo

PROVINSIE WES-KAAP • **PROVINCE OF THE WESTERN CAPE** • **IPHONDO LENTSHONA KOLONI**

---

22 July 2002

Dear Mr Trovato

COMPLAINT: TRAIN SERVICE IN CAPE TOWN

By direction of Mr P Meyer MPP, Minister of Health, I acknowledge receipt of your letter dated 3 July 2002.

Kindly note that the above-mentioned documentation has been referred to Ms T Essop, Minister of Transport (t) 483 2171, for her attention and finalisation.

Kind regards

HERMAN VAN DER WESTHUIZEN
HEAD: OFFICE OF THE MINISTER

Mr Ben Trovato
PO Box 1117
Sea Point
8060

3 July, 2002

Dear Commissioner,

Congratulations on the fine job you are doing. I have not seen a single crime committed before my eyes in almost two months. There was a time that we were unable to move without tripping over a rapist or murderer. In fact, the only crime I have witnessed lately was when the National Party's Marthinus van Schalkwyk stole the job of premier! My neighbour was so outraged that he wanted to lay charges of theft. I managed to convince him to stay out of it and pretend that he saw nothing.

Even though you appear to have crime well under control, I am concerned about the younger generation. They do not seem to possess the values that have been instilled in men like you and I. This morning I was going for a stroll along the Sea Point promenade when I came across two teenagers openly kissing on a bench! I am no prude and have done my fair share of canoodling. But always in the privacy of my own home. It seems that even smooching has changed since our days. At first, I thought the girl on the promenade had passed out and was being given mouth-to-mouth resuscitation, such was the frantic urgency with which he was setting about her. Had an alien from outer space landed just then, he would have thought this was a planet of people who ate one another.

You may have read in the paper the other day that the Iranian police arrested 30 girls and boys during what they called a "depraved" birthday party. It turned out that the youngsters were dancing with each other. As you know, this is not allowed under sharia law. That is what makes Islam such a wholesome religion. The youngsters were given fines, suspended jail sentences and up to 70 lashes each. It may sound a little on the harsh side, but these kids will certainly think twice before engaging in such degenerate behaviour in the future.

Dancing may appear to be an innocent pursuit to many of us. But, just as dagga leads to heroin, mixed-gender dancing leads to unprotected sex and Satanism. And the Iranians know this better than most.

Would it be possible for your men to step up their raids on parties in some of our residential areas? I know of several homes near me that are used for drinking and dancing over weekends. I will provide the addresses if you can guarantee me protection.

Down with hedonism!

Yours truly,

Ben Trovato (Mr)

South African Police Service   *Suid-Afrikaanse Polisiediens*

| Private Bag
Privaatsak | X9004, CAPE TOWN / KAAPSTAD, 8000 | Fax :
Faks : | (021) 417-7336 |

15 July 2002

Dear Mr. Trovato

YOUR LETTER DATED 3 JULY 2002

1. On behalf of the Provincial Commissioner, I hereby acknowledge receipt of your letter dated as above. The Commissioner has noted the content thereof with thanks and once again expresses his sincere commitment to the effective combating of crime in the Western Cape.

2. Whilst some, like yourself, may view it as lamentable, our fine constitution does not permit the criminalisation of displays of public affection or dancing and the enjoyment of music. This of course, as long as the former does not amount to public indecency (where nudity is usually a prerequisite) or the latter interfere with the serenity and peace of others. If I may make so bold, I do feel that the punishments which you propose are a trifle harsh, even in view of the intense emotions which the actions in question appear to arouse in you.

3. Nevertheless, please feel free to contact my office should you wish to meet with me in order to discuss your concerns in depth. To this end, my contact details are as follows:

   Tel. (W):(021) 417-7388
   Fax:(021) 417-7389

4. In view of your previous generosity, I gladly enclose R10-00 to cover your travel expenses.

5. Please convey my kindest regards to Brenda and Clive. I trust all is well with the lad.

Yours sincerely,

SUPERINTENDENT
f/PROVINCIAL COMMISSIONER: WESTERN CAPE
M W ROMBURGH

Mr Ben Trovato
PO Box 1117
Sea Point
8060

22 July, 2002

Dear Superintendent Romburgh,

Allow me to congratulate you on your fine police work. You are indeed a sleuth of the first order! In my original letter, I made no mention of my wife or son. And yet you passed on your regards to both Brenda and Clive. It would not surprise me at all to hear that your colleagues refer to you as The Human Bloodhound. It is no wonder that you have made Superintendent. In fact, I shall be writing to the Minister of Safety and Security recommending that he promote you to Inspector General. But please do not get your hopes up. The minister is a Communist and I was trained by this country's finest military theorists to regard these people with extreme prejudice. However, since his first name is Charles and not Vladimir, it is more likely that he only brings out his dog-eared copy of Das Kapital at cocktail parties and not while he is at work.

Clive is now out of the institute and is doing relatively well. I gave him the R10 that you so kindly sent me, and now you are his hero. He says that when he grows up he wants to join the Uninformed Branch. I presume he means Uniformed Branch. He also says that he wants to thank you personally, but this might not be a good idea as I suspect he wants to extort more money out of you so he can buy the latest Eminem album.

I could not help but notice that you are less than enthusiastic about my suggestion regarding the imposition of lashes on youngsters caught flagrantly disregarding all moral sensibilities. As you so rightly point out, the Constitution prevents it. But this only applies while you are in uniform. My neighbour and I are becoming informal vigilantes, much like informal parking attendants but with Hawaiian shirts and more muscle. We would be honoured if you joined us on one of our outings. Ted's wife, Mary, provides the snacks and Brenda does the drinks. The risk of poisoning always livens things up a bit! We are a little short on equipment so bring what you can. However, if you are unable to afford a cattle prod, one will be provided for you free of charge.

Best wishes,

....
Ben Trovato (Mr)

PS. A man of your investigative talents should be able to find out Jackie Selebi's real name. Let me know what you get.

Mr Ben Trovato
PO Box 1117
Sea Point
8060

4 July, 2002

The Instructor-in-Chief
Arthur Murray School of Dancing
PO Box 2505
Rivonia
2128

Dear Instructor-in-Chief,

Ever since I was a little boy I have wanted to learn how to dance. I once made the mistake of mentioning this to my father. He got his gun (a Walther PPK), took me outside and started firing into the ground around my feet. When the magazine was empty, he looked at me and said: "See. You don't need lessons."

These days he is too old to shoot straight. Besides, I would never tell him that I am considering joining your outfit. The shock would probably kill him. On second thoughts, perhaps I will tell him. But I am straying from the point. Before I am crippled with arthritis, I need to feel what it is like to swing a woman about on the dance floor. I tried it once with my wife, Brenda, but she thought I was attacking her and chased me through the house with my son's aluminium baseball bat.

 The Arthur Murray School of Dancing is renowned. So it makes sense that I come to you first. But one thing is troubling me. When I mentioned my intentions to my neighbour, he was quick to warn me against it. Ted says that Arthur Murray was responsible for opening up the drug trade in America. He says Murray was the man who made contact with Pablo Escobar and began smuggling tons of cocaine straight out of Bolivia. Not only that, but Murray was also selling guns to both the Medellin and Cali cartels. I asked him if he was sure he had the right Arthur Murray, and he nodded and tapped his nose. Old Ted knows a thing or two, but I wanted to check with you before I sign up with my local dance studio.

Please let me know if your Mr Murray was ever a drug-smuggling gunrunner. Is he still alive? I would hate to find myself involved in a front company for the global narcotics trade.

I anxiously await your response.

Yours truly,

Ben Trovato (Mr)

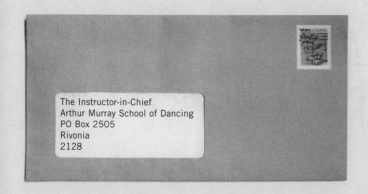

Mr Ben Trovato
PO Box 1117
Sea Point
8060

4 August, 2002

Dear Sir,

It has been a month since I wrote to you enquiring about the possibility of joining one of your schools, and I have not yet had a reply. I know that you expect people to dance to your tune, but that is no reason to ignore us.

If you recall, I had expressed concerns about Mr Murray's background. It has been suggested in certain quarters that your Mr Murray had more than a passing interest in the global drug trade. And that the dancing schools are merely money laundering fronts.

I have managed to convince my wife that we need to learn the foxtrot, the tango and all those other exotic styles that made Fred Astair and Ginger Rogers the most romantic couple in all of Hollywood history. But not at the expense of our freedom.

Once again, I await your assurances that we will not be arrested as accomplices if we join one of Arthur Murray's dancing schools.

Thank you.

Yours truly,

....
Ben Trovato (Mr)

IAN D. McCALLUM
LICENSEE

13th August, 2002

Dear Mr. Trovato,

I refer to your two letters dated 4th July and 4th August which have been passed on to me by my franchisee in Johannesburg.

Firstly I must apologise for the delay in replying but this is due to the fact that on reading your first letter I was completely amazed and bewildered by it's content. On a second reading I was convinced that someone was playing a joke on us. However, I assume this now not to be the case as you have enquired once again.

In the 44 years that I have been part of the Arthur Murray organization I have never once heard any type of insinuation that Mr Arthur Murray was involved in any way whatsoever with the drug trade in America.

I started my Arthur Murray career in London and had the opportunity of meeting both Arthur and Kathryn Murray on a couple of occasions. I have always had tremendous admiration for the man who started the finest social dance organization in the world and can assure you that I would not have had anything to do with a company whose founder had drug smuggling or gunrunning implications.

My late husband Ian McCallum started the Arthur Murray organization here in South Africa in 1955. He was a man of great integrity and honesty and would certainly never have been associated with a company which had a 'shady' history.

You are quite right when you state "the Arthur Murray School of Dancing is renowned". We are, without doubt, the largest and most successful social dance organisation in the world. The A.M. studios in South Africa are held in very high esteem by our head office and board of directors in America.

Over the years our studios in South Africa have taught hundreds of thousands of people to dance. Apart from achieving a high dance standard our students have fun, gain confidence, make new friends and develop a whole new social life. We have always prided ourselves on being a huge Arthur Murray family and in a few cases are presently teaching fourth generation of families.

In view of the high reputation the Arthur Murray organization has here in South Africa and around the world I find it absolutely inconceivable that anyone could associate it with drug smuggling, gun running or money laundering.

However, may I suggest that if you still have reservations concerning Mr. Arthur Murray (who incidentally passed away some years ago) you could contact our Head Office in Coral Gables, Florida. U.S.A. for further assurance.

I am absolutely delighted to hear that both you and your wife would like to take dance lessons with us and, should you decide to do so, I look forward to meeting you in the near future.

We have two Arthur Murray studios in the Cape Town area, one in Bellville and the other in Table View. They are both owned by Mr. & Mrs. Burger Herbst. Mrs. Herbst (known as Miss Lynn) runs the Bellville branch whilst Mr. Herbst runs the Table View studio. They have a wonderful team of proffesional instructors and I know you will be very well taught and looked after.

I suggest you call Miss Lynn on the above telephone number to make an appointment to visit the studio of you choice, to learn more about our activities and to participate in a complimentary half hour lesson for both you and your wife. I can assure you that you are under no obligation to enroll with us if you are hesitant in any way.

May you and your wife have many happy hours of dancing ahead.

Yours sincerely,

SYLVIA McCALLUM
MASTER FRANCHISEE

c.c.Mr. & Mrs. Herbst.

The Manager
Babcock Equipment
PO Box 3498
Johannesburg
2000

Mr Ben Trovato
PO Box 1117
Sea Point
8060

4 July, 2002

Dear Sir,

I am sure you are a busy man, so I will be brief.

I was at a function the other night and overheard a group of men talking about Babcocks. At first I thought they were comparing size, as men are inclined to do after a few drinks. But listening more closely, it turned out that they were in fact discussing something called Babcocks.

To be honest, I have no idea what a Babcock is. I know what a shuttlecock is because I used to play the game with my sister. Everyone knows what a weathercock is for, although I have yet to see one pointing in the right direction. A cockalorum is a self-important little man and a cockatrice is a legendary monster, part snake and part rooster, that can kill with a single glance. It sounds like my wife, Brenda. I know that cockshy refers to a game involving coconuts and not men who avoid public urinals. And I know that a cockabully is a small freshwater fish from New Zealand and a cockup is what happened when Marthinus van Schalkwyk became premier of the Western Cape.

But I do not know what is a Babcock.

I tried to get information from several sources in Cape Town, but down here any mention of the C-word leads to pursed lips and invitations which I could not possibly accept.

Enlighten me, please.

Yours truly,

Ben Trovato (Mr)

GAUTENG
P.O. Box 13902
Witfield 1467
Tel: +27 (011) 826 6511
Fax: +27 (011) 823 2030

KWA-ZULU NATAL
P.O. Box 190
New Germany 3620
Tel: +27 (031) 705 2733/42
Fax: +27 (031) 705 2522

MPUMALANGA
P.O. Box 170
Middelburg 1050
Tel: +27 (013) 246 2867
Fax: +27 (013) 246 2863

WEBSITE: www.babcockpeq.co.za
E-MAIL: enquiries@babcockpeq.co.za

WESTERN CAPE
P16-18 Willow Road
Stikland 7530
Tel: +27 (021) 946 2655
Fax: +27 (021) 946 2656

FREE STATE
P.O. Box 2007
Bloemfontein 9300
Tel: +27 (051) 432 3302
Fax: +27 (051) 432 3351

MPUMALANGA
P.O. Box 5296
Nelspruit 1200
Tel: +27 (013) 755 2130
Fax: +27 (013) 755 1934

25 July 2002

Dear Mr Trovato

I refer to your letter dated 4 July 2002, querying what a Babcock is.

To be quite truthful, we are as confused as you are as to the origin and meaning of a Babcock. The matter gets even more baffling when you consider that our company was originally founded in the USA some 120 years ago under the appellation Babcock & Wilcox. At many board meetings over the years we have pondered whether these gentlemen were the founders of our company, and if so, were they more than just friends?

We have come to recognize that to go on speculating is futile and that by electing to work for Babcock we take on the burden of being made fun of by our competitors and idle gossip mongerers. Maybe the reason why we are so successful and have seen the start of two centuries is that we have been forged through the fires of ridicule and humiliation.

Yours sincerely

FRANK REID
MANAGING DIRECTOR

PS:It is interesting to note that we have often been misnamed as Badcock, which has taken great presence of mind to deal with but in the final analysis we feel that a Willingcock is better than a Badcock or even Nocock at all!

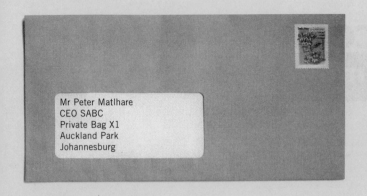

Mr Ben Trovato
PO Box 1117
Sea Point
8060

9 July, 2002

Dear Mr Matlhare,

I wish to complain about the lack of decent pornography on SABC television channels.

Instead, we get endless moronic soaps featuring people with names like Jade and Sasha. That is if we aren't being forced to sit through documentaries on the mating habits of the endangered Amazonian screwworm.

Sir, the spark has gone out of my marriage. My conjugal rights continue to be violated and I am at the end of my tether. Brenda (my wife) needs to be snapped out of her celibate state. I am convinced that a bit of porn on the old telly would do the trick. She has to be reminded that other people still engage in this practice. And that coitus is not something played on the deck of a cruise ship.

Every night, I try to keep Brenda in front of the television for as long as possible in the hope of catching a glimpse of some gratuitous copulating. I once heard of a programme called Fellatio, which sounded promising. But it turned out to be a talk show involving some dreadful woman with a similar name.

As the man in charge of the public broadcaster, I am sure you have the power to instruct one of the channels to begin showing more sex. Not just a flash of thigh, but the real rumpy pumpy stuff. And not too late in the evening, please. I tend to nod off around ten.

Please let me know if you are prepared to help save my marriage.

Thank you and God bless.

Yours truly,

Ben Trovato (Mr)

PS. Enclosed please find R10 to help speed up the process.

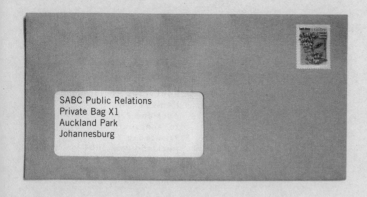

Mr Ben Trovato
PO Box 1117
Sea Point
8060

23 August, 2002

Dear Sir or Madam:

I wrote to the SABC on the 9th of July and have not yet had a response. As a person who diligently pays his television licence, I am outraged by your capacity to ignore people.

You may recall that I was enquiring about the possibility of the SABC showing programmes of a more adult nature. I am not talking about Days of our Lives, here. Think Emmanuel with less dialogue and fewer clothes. There are many people of my generation who need their marriages spiced up by something a little raunchier than Dawson's Creek.

As licence-payers, you are obliged to listen to us. Let me know if you plan on doing something about it.

Let's hear from you this time.

Yours truly,

....
Ben Trovato (Mr)

PS. Any idea what might have happened to my ten rand that I sent along to help speed up the process? You might want to check Mr Matlare's top drawer.

S∧BC
AUDIENCE LIAISON
Corporate Affairs

Room 2302 Radiopark
Henley Road
Auckland Park
Johannesburg
Private Bag X1
Auckland Park 2006
Tel: 27 11 714-5178/3821
Fax: 27 11 714-4508
e-mail: moan@sabc.co.za

30 August 2002

Dear Mr Trovato

Thank you for your letters of 9 July and 23 August. The second of these was delivered to the Labour Relations department, and the postal worker who showed such initiative is being considered for promotion. I apologise for taking so long to reply to your first letter. The delay was occasioned by deliberations at executive level on the possibility of granting your request, and on the best use of your contribution. Ultimately, however, the consensus was that since the SABC already screens so much pornography, expending a further ten rand on it would simply be an extravagance. I therefore regretfully return your R10 note, although we were tempted to use it to buy another season of Dawson's Creek.

I have gathered from your letter that you believe there is no hard pornography on our television channels, so I can only conclude that you have been watching at the wrong time. Unlike other broadcasters, who believe that pornography belongs in the small hours, we have been innovative and placed it mainly in the morning. Our research has shown that many married people tend to nod off around ten at night, which might be at the root of their celibate state, so we like to catch them when they are still invigorated and the kids are off to school. Just to give you a taste of what is on offer during the day:

- The Little Mermaid: a titillating young siren, if somewhat fishy. Perhaps not as stimulating for Brenda, but Neptune does some interesting things with his trident.
- Aladdin: getting it off on a wild magic carpet ride.
- Bare in the Big Blue House: you may have been misled by the spelling error ('Bear') in the title, for which we apologise. Blue, as the title indicates.
- Black Beauty: for those who like to add some colour to spice the conjugal encounter.
- Dragonballz: a must for Brenda. This is in the afternoon, placed specially for women whose partners would like a hot (as opposed to lukewarm) welcome home.

Perhaps a simple change of viewing habits would do the trick. We wish you many happy returns of your conjugal rights.

Yours sincerely

DOROTHY VAN TONDER
DOROTHY VAN TONDER
Manager: Compliance & Liaison
Policy & Regulatory Affairs

PS You might want to check whether Henry Root has copyrighted his original concept. If so, this R10 may well come in handy.

Mr Ben Trovato
PO Box 1117
Sea Point
8060

9 July, 2002

Dear Sir,

I hope you are able to assist me.

My neighbour and I popped into your fine establishment one morning about a week ago for a quick snort to give the day a little more clarity. Unfortunately, we overstayed our welcome. As far as I recall, dinner was about to be served by the time a friendly member of your staff showed us to the parking lot.

Since then I have been accosted by my wife demanding to know where the garden gnome has got to. Then it struck me. I had taken the gnome along to your hotel, but he failed to return home with me. I cannot say for sure what possessed me to bring him along for a drink, but I dare say the idea made sense at the time.

He is just under a metre high (tall for a gnome) and as last seen wearing a pointy red hat and blue lederhosen. He had a fishing rod, but my friend tells me that I was using it as a swizzle stick so it may no longer be attached to his hand.

Quite frankly, I could not care less about the gnome. But my wife insists that I find it. She seems to think that it has some kind of sentimental value because her sister's husband gave it to us as a wedding gift. I have always thought that as far as presents go, giving someone a garden gnome is the same as giving someone a voucher for a free consultation with a physician who specialises in sexual dysfunction. This probably explains why Brenda spends more time with the gnome than she does with me. Although I am sure that their relationship is nothing more than platonic, she seems to miss Little Big Man (her name, not mine).

Please could you check with your lost property people to see if they have our gnome?

Thank you.

Yours truly,

Ben Trovato (Mr)

MOUNT NELSON HOTEL

100 YEARS

1899 - 1999

2 August 2002

Dear Mr Trovato

RE: GARDEN GNOME:

Thank you for your letter dated 9 July 2002.

Unfortunately after having checked all possible areas and spoken to relevant staff members, we have been unable to trace your missing garden gnome.

Should we find "Little Big Man" we will be in direct contact with you. Sorry that we cannot respond with better news.

Yours sincerely

Odette Arbuthnot
PA to Hotel Manager

Mr Ben Trovato
PO Box 1117
Sea Point
8060

9 July, 2002

Dear Sir,

Your resort comes highly recommended. A friend of minor Italian nobility said if there is one place on earth that he would want to die, it is Sabi Sabi. Personally, I am in no rush to die. But I suppose if one were seeking an early death, one would choose a place that is full of dangerous man-eating animals. One would not, for example, recommend a health spa as the best place in which to die, no matter how luxurious the surroundings.

But getting back to business. I urgently need to take my wife, Brenda, away for a week. The pilot light of my marriage has gone out. The geyser is cold. But I still have gas in me. Plenty of it. All I need is a spark. The explosion is guaranteed. And I suspect that Sabi Sabi could well prove to be my personal Ground Zero. However, before I make a reservation, there are certain things on which I need clarity.

Since the pilot light has been extinguished, I will need fuel to stoke the fire. In my case, this means role-playing. When I was courting Brenda, she once asked me to dress up as a Rastafarian bongo player. I arrived at her house wearing a Caribbean print shirt and imitation dreadlocks, not really knowing what to expect. It wasn't long before she began playing Bob Marley tunes and plying me with a powerful rum punch. Later, she rolled a marijuana cigarette and brought out a drum from beneath her bed. To be honest, it was the best evening of my life.

But that was before the Ice Age descended. Now, Brenda needs to be coaxed back into the tropics. And what better place to do it than surrounded by the eroticism of the bush?

Before I make a reservation, I thought it only fair to check with you whether there will be any problems. Even though my Italian friend tells me that Sabi Sabi is a very liberal place, I would not want to be confronted by heavily armed khaki-clad game rangers just as the fun begins. My plan is to pick up the bongos on the second or third night. It's best to give Brenda a chance to settle in before I turn on the power. I assume that you have marijuana on the premises. Or would you suggest I bring my own? I realise there is a chance that the Rastafarian game may no longer work. As a precaution, I will bring along my Raging Bull outfit. It worked in Pamplona many years ago, and there is no reason why it should not work at Sabi Sabi. All I need is a clear run of about 20 metres.

Please let me know if my needs are acceptable to management, as I have to book soon.

Yours truly,

Ben Trovato (Mr)

SABI SABI

24 July 2002

Dear Mr Trovato

Thank you for considering Sabi Sabi for your special romantic weekend. We are able to offer you our Rhino Horn suite, consisting of a very large bedroom, luxurious bathroom with sunken double jacuzzi and sumptuous lounge, all interconnected by a 30 metre passage. This, we feel, would more than adequately accommodated for your Pamplona bull run, (or "buffalo" run, as we prefer to call it).

As far as your request for Marijuana is concerned, we at Sabi Sabi are particularly concerned about conservation and ecology, and to this end, no exotic shrubs are either planted, cooked, eaten or smoked on the property. However, through extensive research, we have identified a number of indigenous plants and herbs, such as Bushman's Tea (Cathaedulis) and Sausage Tree (Kigelia Africana), which experienced guests, such as yourself, have informed us are infinitely more potent than marijuana. We will be happy to supply you with as much of these as you feel you may need.

Although you expressed a degree of negativity towards health spas, may we take the liberty of advising you of the benefits of our Earth Nature Spa for your specific needs? We believe that our specially trained therapists and masseurs will make your stay with us even more memorable, and take some of the pressure off yourself. The treatment we recommend consists of a detoxifying and energizing seaweed wrap, after which you and Brenda would soak in a double hydro jet bath before being given our ultimate sensual massage in our twin massaging room. You would both be brought to the brink of pleasure at which time we would bundle you off to your suite. This could save you a lot of energy, and would also avoid your having to pack at least one Rastafarian style outfit in your luggage.

Please let us know if there is anything else we could do to make your stay at Sabi Sabi more combustible.

Yours faithfully

Patrick Shorten

Mr P Shorten
MANAGING DIRECTOR

Mr Ben Trovato
PO Box 1117
Sea Point
8060

12 July, 2002

Dear Sir,

I trust that everything is in place for the United Nations World Summit on Sustainable Development? With sixty thousand delegates heading for Gauteng, the most important thing is to provide a sustainable supply of food and alcohol. If these essential resources are depleted, delegates are likely to wander off in search of something a little more substantial than endless debates. And the one thing you do not want in Johannesburg is to have the visitors wandering off on their own.

What do you intend doing about the Nigerians? Have you given any thought to how the foreign delegates are likely to react to being jostled and harassed by hordes of illegal immigrants trying to sell them everything from crack cocaine to plastic sunglasses?

The African delegates will feel quite at home, but I fear a terrible shock awaits anyone coming from places like Stockholm. Nobody rubs up against you in Gamlastan and tries to sell you Rolex watches with the silver flaking off. Nor does someone come along seconds later and threaten to chop your head off with a blunt panga unless you hand over the watch. And your shoes.

I am sure that most delegates would prefer to concentrate on the issues at hand, and not be distracted by people who want money, food and their cellphones. After all, this is precisely why the lower classes have been excluded from the conference.

I plan on being in Johannesburg next month and will be available for a day or two to protect small groups of delegates should they wish to venture further than the conference centre. All I need is accreditation and a supply of AA batteries for my cattle prod.

Enclosed please find ten rand to facilitate matters.

Yours truly,

Ben Trovato (Mr)

BRIBE GIVEN R10

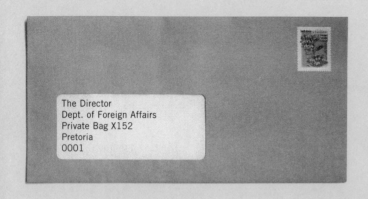

Mr Ben Trovato
PO Box 1117
Sea Point
8060

7 August, 2002

Dear Sir,

I have not yet received a reply to my letter dated 12th July, and time is running out.

You may recall that I was offering to provide protection to First World delegates coming to South Africa for the World Summit on Sustainable Development.

I also sent you money to facilitate my accreditation.

Not only do I not have my accreditation, but I am also R10 down.

Please can you find out what is going on. I would not want to arrive in Johannesburg with all my equipment only to find my way barred by thugs wearing Secret Service sunglasses and earpieces.

You may use the address at the top of this page. The one on the right-hand side.

Thank you.

Yours truly,

Ben Trovato (Mr)

DEPARTMENT: FOREIGN AFFAIRS
REPUBLIC OF SOUTH AFRICA
Private Bag X152, Pretoria, 0001, Tel: (012) 351 1000

16 August 2002

Dear Mr Trovato

I refer to your letters dated 12 July and 7 August 2002.

The comments in your letter have been noted.

We wish to advise that we will not be able to make use of your services and therefore return your Ten Rand (enclosed).

Yours sincerely

Dayanand Naidoo
Director: International Conferences

Mr Andries Viljoen
CEO: South African Airways
Private Bag X13
Johannesburg Int. Airport
1627

Mr Ben Trovato
PO Box 1117
Sea Point
8060

17 July, 2002

Dear Mr Viljoen,

My wife and I are frequent fliers. I have family in Palermo and friends in Northern Ireland. Brenda has business associates in Lagos and her father lives in Monaco. We also have holiday homes in Venice and Portugal.

South African Airways has always been our carrier of choice. Brenda and I have never been anything but satisfied with the service. The only exception was during a trip to London when a steward reached for my tray and "accidentally" grabbed my willy instead.

We are due for a trip soon and I was about to call my travel agent when my neighbour, Ted, said that he hoped we got there safely now that SAA had begun hiring pilots from the township. He was surprised to hear that I did not know about your new policy. He said there is one man who worked as a baggage handler at Lesotho Airways and who is now the captain of an SAA jumbo jet.

I am not a racist, but Brenda is decidedly nervous about flying overseas on an aircraft captained by a man who might have been up all night beating his wife and carousing in a shebeen.

I could not care less what he does in his personal life, but I have seen how these people drive taxis and I doubt that my heart is strong enough to survive fourteen hours of swerving violently across the Atlantic. Even if he does it in nine. Just the thought of cutting in front of other planes on the airstrip makes me nervous.

Do you think we should take a chance on your chap from the location, or would you advise that we switch airlines for safety's sake? I suppose there would not be much chance of a darkie getting into a Swiss Air cockpit. From what I hear, they are not even allowed into the country.

We would appreciate your suggestions as soon as possible.

Yours truly,

Ben Trovato (Mr)

Mr Andries Viljoen
CEO: South African Airways
Private Bag X13
Johannesburg Int. Airport
1627

Mr Ben Trovato
PO Box 1117
Sea Point
8060

7 August, 2002

Dear Mr Viljoen,

I have not heard from you in connection with my query dated 17th July. However, I am sure your response has gone astray in the mail since SAA can hardly afford to alienate loyal customers like Brenda and I.

If you recall, I was seeking assurances that it is safe to fly with one of your darker-skinned pilots. Since then, my fears have been exacerbated by the news that one of your Previously Disadvantaged Pilots was caught with a mound of Bolivian cocaine in his underwear. I appreciate that he may well be telling the truth when he says he does not know how it got there. Do you know how it got there? Are you planning to introduce random testing for staff?

The idea that your pilots indulge in sex-soaked drug orgies the moment they reach cruising altitude does not inspire confidence in the airline.

Once again, I ask for your assurance that it is safe to fly with SAA pilots who might be other than white, whether they be drugged or not.

Thank you.

Yours truly,

....
Ben Trovato (Mr)

SOUTH AFRICAN
AIRWAYS

07 August 2002

Dear Mr Trovato

André Viljoen, President and CEO of South African Airways, has shared your letter, dated 17 July 2002, and has requested that I respond on his behalf.

Mr Trovato, it seems to us that you have been misled through wrong information which could cause a serious adverse effect upon South African Airways. I just happen to have a copy of our Wings edition where we announced the first appointment of our very qualified black Captain, Mpho Mamashela. I am enclosing a copy of this report. You will see that Captain Mamashela is a fully qualified pilot and through his commitment to aviation and personal success he managed to become one of our best pilots through skill, enthusiasm and passion.

Mr Trovato, you and your wife can rest assured that South African Airways have some of the best pilots in the world on our team. The safety of our passengers, crew and aircraft is never compromised. You also have our assurance that although the air traffic may at times be busy, that it is nothing similar and cannot be compared to the rush hour traffic or manner in which our taxis operate on the roads.

Thank you for taking the time to write to us. Mr Trovato, in this day and age the colour of a person does not label a man and we hope that you will see things from a different perspective and support our decision to have someone as well credited as Captain Mpho Mamashela, and others like him.

With kind regards

Gillian Watts
EXECUTIVE OFFICE – SOUTH AFRICAN AIRWAYS

SOUTH AFRICAN
AIRWAYS

14 August 2002

Dear Mr. Trovato

Thank you for your letter dated 7 August 2002. We so happened to respond to your original concerns on the same date and have pleasure in forwarding a copy of our reply.

The recent incident involving one of our pilots was an unfortunate one indeed and will be dealt with the seriousness it deserves. Safety at South African Airways is of paramount importance and will not be compromised at any cost. You have my emphatic assurance that all precautions humanly possible are taken to ensure the safety of you, our valued customer, our crew and equipment at all times. For obvious reasons we cannot elaborate on what measures we take to prevent an occurrence such as the one under correspondence.

We at South African Airways sincerely value your custom and trust that we can look forward to your continued support.

Kind regards

Michael van Niekerk
Senior Manager
CUSTOMER RELATIONS

The Director
SA Brain Research Institute
6 Campbell Street
Waverley
Johannesburg

Mr Ben Trovato
PO Box 1117
Sea Point
8060

17 July, 2002

Dear Sir,

I am sure you are a very busy man, so I will get straight to the point.

I would like to donate my brain. Not immediately, of course. But once I die, it is all yours. I imagine that you do not get many offers like this, so you must be very excited.

It is a fine brain, I assure you. Many of my friends have grown dimwitted with age and alcohol abuse. As a man of moderation, I am proud to say that mine remains in perfect working order. And I take good care of it, too. Whenever my wife and I have an argument, I am quick to strap on a kevlar cycling helmet to ensure that the cranium remains in one piece. There are many, many men out there who have clearly suffered one too many blows to the head. Some are in prison, some are in parliament. I need not tell you, of all people, that science has little use for addled brains.

Naturally, my brain is no longer the Porsche that it once was. These days it is more like a station wagon – a family brain that is slightly worn from years of trying to squeeze in too many people and a wet dog at the same time. But the synapses still crackle like a log fire on a winter's night in Cape Town.

In return for my brain, all I ask is that you help resolve an issue that has been troubling me. A friend of mine in America (he is a Harvard graduate currently spending some time in a state facility in Colorado) referred me to an MIT man by the name of Marvin Minsky on this same issue. Here it is. How long will it take before scientists are able to download human consciousness into a machine? Minsky says it will happen.

On my demise, would you like someone to courier my brain to you? If so, would it be acceptable to send the entire head? I doubt that any of my friends would be prepared to perform the retrieval procedure. Alternatively, you may wish to collect it personally, in which case I will give you my home address. Mind you, there is no guarantee that this is where I will shuffle off the mortal coil. It could be down the road at the post office. But if Brenda has her way, you are more than likely to find my body at home. For your sake, I hope she uses poison and not a blunt instrument. Bludgeoning could ruin everything.

I look forward to hearing from you.

Yours truly,

Ben Trovato (Mr)

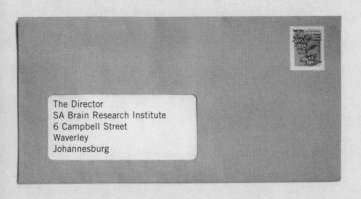

Mr Ben Trovato
PO Box 1117
Sea Point
8060

7 August, 2002

Dear Sir,

I have not yet received a reply to my letter of 17th July. I assume it has gone astray in the mail, since I find it unlikely that you would ignore a man who is prepared to donate his brain in the name of science.

Did you manage to come up with an answer to the Minsky prediction?

You may be pleased to know that I am cutting back on the whisky so that my brain is not too damaged by the time you harvest it. If you are not interested in my offer, please let me know so that I can resume my regular intake. There is no point in depriving oneself needlessly.

Hope to hear from you soon.

Yours truly,

Ben Trovato (Mr)

PS. I am including a stamp in case you have run out.

Mr Ben Trovato
PO Box 1117
Sea Point
8060

7 August 2002

The Director
SA Brain Research Institute
6 Campbell Street
Waverley
Johannesburg

Dear Sir,

I have not yet received a reply to my letter of 17th July. I assume it has gone astray in the mail, since I find it unlikely that you would ignore a man who is prepared to donate his brain in the name of science.

Did you manage to come up with an answer to the Minsky prediction?

You may be pleased to know that I am cutting back on the whisky so that my brain is not too damaged by the time you harvest it. If you are not interested in my offer, please let me know so that I can resume my regular intake. There is no point in depriving oneself needlessly.

Hope to hear from you soon.

Yours truly,

Ben Trovato (Mr)

PS. I am including a stamp in case you have run out.

13/08/02

We do not take Brain Donations - you should donate it rather to the Anatomy Dept @ UCT

118

Mr Ben Trovato
PO Box 1117
Sea Point
8060
Cape Town
South Africa

22 July, 2002

Dear Sir,

My wife and I are planning a second honeymoon. The first was a complete disaster and we are still paying compensation to a young couple from Stockholm. But this is not your concern and I will not bore you with the details.

I had been considering the possibility of sailing to Thailand on the family yacht, but that would have taken too long. Knowing my wife, the honeymoon would be over before we had even passed Mauritius. And I am sure the last thing Thailand needs is another frustrated middle-aged white couple causing a scene in your country.

Actually, we began arguing the moment I raised the idea of a second honeymoon. She wanted to go to Australia, I wanted to go to Jamaica. She wanted to go to Bulgaria, I wanted to go to Spain. She said Morocco, I said Madagascar. You get the idea. After hours of dispute, she said "Phuket" and walked out of the room.

I checked the map, and there you were, Phuket. But when I tried to make enquiries at my local travel agent, they called security and had me escorted to the door. My neighbour suggested that I might be pronouncing the name incorrectly. But he changed his tune when I made mention of "philosophy" and "philanderer" and "phallus" and "pharmacology" and "photocopier" and "Phrixus", the son of Athamus and Nephele who escaped the wrath of his father's mistress, Ino, by flying to Colchis on a winged ram with a golden fleece.

I have considered various resorts, but the name Banyan Tree appeals to me. Do you, in fact, have a banyan tree on the premises or is it simply the name that you chose on the assumption that not even foreigners could get it wrong? But that is not important. What is important, is that you have a honeymoon suite that can rekindle the flame of passion that once burned brightly in my Brenda's bosom. I have always found that moonlight on the ocean works well up to a point. Do you have a suite that overlooks the beach? And what about your staff? Are there any nice Italians among them? Even though I have Italian blood, I have always found that people from Naples especially are unable to keep their hands to themselves. And that counts for everything from diamond tiaras to your wife's bottom.

I am looking at three weeks in October. Let me know what you have, but be quick.

Dr Ben Trovato

BANYAN TREE
----PHUKET----

12 August, 2002

To: Dr. Ben Trovato
From: Maitree Yaipun
No. of pages:1
Subject: Room rate April 01 – Nov 01'02

Dear Dr. Ben Trovato,

Thank you very much for your letter. We are appreciated for your interesting in our resort for your second honey moon. We are pleased to confirm the availability of villas for the mentioned period at the following rates:

Jacuzzi Villa	US$336, Lagoon Jacuzzi Villa	US$400
Pool Villa	US$560, Lagoon Pool Villa	US$640
Spa Pool Villa	US$800, Two Bed Room Pool Villa	US$950

Rates are quoted per villa per night on room only basis and subject to 10% service charge, 7% government tax and 1% provincial tax. The maximum of guests per villa is three, except for Two Bed Room Pool Villa maximum of five person. Extra bed can be provided at US$35 per night plus service charge and tax. Kindly be informed that Spa Pool Villa is for two person stay only. We certainly have the banyan trees in our place, the villas are very nice furnished and special for honey mooner. We are sorry regarding to Italian staff that that you mentioned because we do not have any available.

To confirm the reservation, kindly advice the room type and credit card number with expiration again.

If you have any questions or require any further information, please do not hesitate to contact us. We look forward to hearing from you.

Best regards,

Maitree Yaipun

Reservations Department
Please visit our website at http://www.banyantree.com

Mr Ben Trovato
PO Box 1117
Sea Point
8060
Cape Town
South Africa

23 July, 2002

Dear Sir,

My wife and I are planning to be in Europe this summer. We met many years ago at the Running of the Bulls in Pamplona, although she was so drunk that she cannot remember a thing. Even today, she still thinks I should be somebody else.

I am arranging an itinerary to take in several of Europe's most romantic cities. You will probably agree that Amsterdam is not among them. The reason I wish to visit your city has more to do with the Dutch government's attitude towards narcotics. Do not get me wrong. I am not an international drug fiend. However, Brenda has led a sheltered life and I feel that now is the time to introduce her to something a little more on the wild side. Please be assured that I have no intention of holing up in your hotel with piles of heroin and hard-core pornography. Russian tourists are known for this kind of behaviour, but not independently wealthy South Africans from good families.

As it will be our second honeymoon, I was hoping to get Brenda to smoke a little marijuana. You will appreciate that I am not able to do this in my own country. I cannot risk having a platoon of heavily armed police officers bursting into my home and setting their vicious man-eating dogs loose on the family. Unlike in your civilised country, the use of relatively harmless narcotics in South Africa will land you in prison where black men will ravage you with their enormous members. I understand that some men actually pay for this kind of thing, but I can assure you that I am not one of them.

Your hotel has been recommended to me by friends in the government. I did not ask them whether you provided guests with marijuana for recreational purposes, but there was an implication that I would be able to get whatever I wished. Again, let me assure me that I will not be requiring bags of the stuff. One or two rolled cigarettes, what we call zols in our country, will be sufficient to get Brenda to loosen up enough to participate in the occasion.

I plan to be in Amsterdam in the latter half of September. Please let me know if your finest suite would be available around that time. I can include the cost of the marijuana in a deposit, if required. The money can be transferred within an hour.

Looking forward to hearing from you.

Yours truly,

....
Dr Ben Trovato

Amsterdam,

Dear Dr. Trovato,

Thank you very much for your interest in Blakes Hotel Amsterdam.

In regards to you letter, I would like to inform you that the use of Marijuna is indeed since several years legalized in the Netherlands. However the sale of all soft-drugs is only permitted in the destinated Coffeeshops, well controlled by our government.

As an hotelier I am able to offer you several Suites, which we still have available in the later half of September. My concierge team will be pleased to direct you to the finest coffeeshops in town, but not able to buy you any soft-drugs.

If you would like to make a reservation for one of our finest suites, please call our Reservations department at: +31-20-5302010 or via e-mail: hotel@blakes.nl

Please feel free to contact me if you have any questions regarding the above.

Kind regards,

Richard van Batenburg
General Manager

Mr Ben Trovato
PO Box 1117
Sea Point
8060
Cape Town
South Africa

23 July, 2002

Dear Sir,

I am interested in reserving your finest suite or a week in the latter half of September. It will be a special occasion since my wife and I are travelling around the world on our second honeymoon. I thought I would include Romania on our itinerary since it has such a violent and romantic history. Much like my marriage, actually.

Your hotel was recommended by a good friend who serves in my government. Normally, I would take his advice without a moment's hesitation. However, he is also a high-ranking member of the South African Communist Party. And given Romania's past, I am not altogether sure if I should trust his judgement in this case.

It seems just the other day that President Nicolae Ceausescu unleashed the troops on unsuspecting tourists in the middle of Bucharest. My neighbour tells me that Ceausescu's execution was faked, and that he is hiding out in the Carpathian Mountains waiting to make his move. He could even be hiding somewhere in your hotel. Have you checked the basement? I am capable of taking care of myself, but I know Brenda would object to having our stay disrupted by mobs of drug-crazed socialists hell-bent on revenge.

And what about King Michael? Unless I am mistaken, he has a score or two of his own to settle. I do not want to be sitting down to breakfast when the hotel is overrun by vicious crypto-communists and embittered royalists. It would spoil the mood.

I read in the paper the other day that a charming fellow by the name of Nicole Mischie, head of the Party of Social Democracy, was threatening to chop the legs off any journalist who dared report that there was corruption in the ruling party. I do not have a problem with this. If your journalists are anything like ours, they deserve to be dismembered. But Mischie should simply offer them free lunches twice a week. It is easier to clean up afterwards and just as effective.

Please let me know if you are expecting an uprising of any kind before September. If not, keep a week open at the end of the month. As I said, nothing but the finest suite will do.

Yours truly,

....
Dr Ben Trovato

Athénée Palace Hilton
Bucharest

6 August 2002

Bucharest

Dear Dr. Trovato,

Many thanks for your letter dated 23 July. We would be very happy to welcome you and Mrs. Trovato to the Athénée Palace Hilton Bucharest in late September. We have a variety of suites for you to decide upon should your travel plans firm up.

While I can not answer your letter point for point in an official letter from us, suffice it to say you certainly brightened my day, and put a smile on my face as well as on the face of our PA, Mariana Eremia. We would be happy to assist you with your plans in September, you just need to be a bit more specific with dates and requirements. While no uprisings or coups are planned, one never knows, and should one begin, the Athénée Palace would certainly be the place to be.

Looking forward to hearing from you again in the near future, we all remain at you disposal for any assistance you may require.

Sincerely,

Robert G. Krygsman
Director of Operations
DO_Bucharest@hilton.com

Gilfillan & Scott-
Berning Art Consultants
PO Box 72126
Parkview
Johannesburg

Mr Ben Trovato
PO Box 1117
Sea Point
8060

24 July, 2002

Dear Sir or Madam:

I was helping an old friend to clean out his attic the other day when we came across a trunk that belonged to his grandfather. Inside it was a painting of a nude lady astride some kind of animal. It could be a horse. We were very excited by this discovery. On closer inspection we noticed that it was signed "Von Gog". My friend immediately began shrieking and falling about, insisting that this must be the same Vincent von Gog who got so drunk that he cut off his own nose. That's the Germans for you!

If this is so, then the picture is probably worth quite a lot. However, I seem to remember that this Von Gog painted flowers, not ladies sitting with legs akimbo on strange looking beasts. I may have him mixed up with someone else, though. There was a French bloke, Gorgon, I think his name was, who used to paint naked ladies. But this is definitely a Von Gog original, and not a Gorgon.

Do you think I should send it to Christie's in New York? I dare say a decent auctioneer could fetch a pretty penny for this piece of work. My friend wanted to sell it at the flea market this weekend so that we could go to Grandwest Casino to gamble and drink beer. But I told him he was being a damn fool and threatened to tell his wife about Mirabelle the bartender.

Anyway, please let me know what I should do.

Yours truly,

Ben Trovato (Mr)

Dear Sir,

I have not yet had a reply to my letter of 24th July. I expect it has gone astray in the mail since I assume you are not in the habit of ignoring potential customers.

If you recall, I was enquiring whether you would be interested in taking a look at a Von Gog original that I discovered in a friend's attic. It is oil on canvas and clearly very old.

Should I forward a photograph of the piece or will you be sending someone down to Cape Town to take a look?

Let me know soon because my friend seems to think we are wasting out time dealing with you.

Yours truly,

Ben Trovato (Mr)

GILFILLAN SCOTT-BERNING

FINE AND DECORATIVE ARTS CONSULTANTS

5 September 2002

Dear Mr. Trovato

Thank you very much for your letter of 23 August 2002 regarding your friend's original picture, possibly by Van Gogh. We would be more than delighted to look at your picture on our next visit to Cape Town. In the meantime, we would be grateful if you could forward a photograph of the picture and a detail of the signature to our Johannesburg address.

Please would you let us have a contact telephone number so that we can contact you directly?

Yours sincerely,

Gillian Scott-Berning

Mr Ben Trovato
PO Box 1117
Sea Point
8060

28 July, 2002

Dear Sir,

I heard from a normally reliable source that it is possible for members of the public to purchase lions from your park. I am interested in doing business with you.

As a fellow South African, I need not tell you that crime is out of control. Just the other day, a bandit stole my cellphone while I was sitting in my car in the middle of a conversation waiting for the lights to change. Then he pulled out a gun, pointed it at me and demanded that I buy the phone back for R100! Needless to say, I paid up. It all happened so quickly that I was able to continue my conversation. Anyway, I am sure you have your own horror stories to tell.

It is my personal security at home that I am more concerned about. I have been robbed nine times in the past year. Watchdogs are no use. They are either shot or simply get stolen along with the TV and video recorder.

I have come to the conclusion that a lion is the answer to my problems. I understand our border police are already using them on Mozambicans who jump the fence. Naturally, I will have to spend some time with it so that it gets to know me. Would you suggest I get a cub, and let it grow up with me like that Adamson fellow in Born Free? To be honest, I would prefer something that already knows how to use its teeth and claws. I believe you have a few white lions in stock. Does this make them friendlier towards white people? A lion genetically programmed to see off the darkies would be ideal.

I was thinking that a male might be a good idea, but I wouldn't want it spraying the entire house every time it felt insecure. You know what cats are like!

Please could you provide me with quotes for a cub and a fully-grown male. I would also appreciate a list of dietary requirements. I don't think my wife, Brenda, would appreciate having the fridge stuffed with Zebra carcasses oozing blood all over the veggies. What about those pellets that they give to really big dogs?

Thank you for your trouble.

Yours truly,

Ben Trovato (Mr)

P O Box 50432
Colleen Glen
6018
Tel: (041) 378 1702
Fax: (041) 378 1703

16 August, 2002

Dear Mr Trovato,

Many thanks for your letter of the 28th, July 2002. I am indeed sorry to read of your woes but, regretably, advise that I am unable to accommodate you with a lion regardless of how desirable the prospect of owning one might be.

Whilst the reasons for this are many, I will spend a few moments enumerating the important ones;

1. Lions are exceedingly dangerous animals that grow to huge proportions weighing between 200/250 kg apiece.

2. They consume large amounts of meat, approx. 40 Kg of fresh horse or donkey meat a week. As carnivores they only eat meat.

3. Special enclosures are required to accommodate them. These have to meet specific standards and need to be fully electrified.

4. They are very expensive – adults cost between R30,000.00 – R150,000.00 depending on the lion.

5. This is probably the most important factor. You will need a permit to hold a lion and this will not be given to a layman residing in subhurbia. In fact, there is a moratorium in place on the granting of permits, which is unlikely to be lifted in the near future. This is the reason why there are so few licenced breeders in the country.

Sorry that I cannot help and trust that you find some solution to your repeated burglaries.

Yours sincerely

R S Gibb

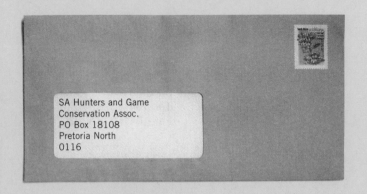

Mr Ben Trovato
PO Box 1117
Sea Point
8060

28 July, 2002

SA Hunters and Game
Conservation Assoc.
PO Box 18108
Pretoria North
0116

Dear Sir,

I am relatively new to the hunting game. Since purchasing my 12-gauge shotgun, all I have managed to bag are two chacma baboons that were scavenging in garbage bins near Scarborough. They look magnificent on my study wall. The taxidermist managed to change their startled expressions into something more akin to the snarling, savage brutes that they really are. Visitors are astounded that I managed to escape with my life.

However, I need something more challenging. There is not much point in messing about with kudu and gemsbok. All they do is stand there with grass hanging out of their mouths, waiting to be shot through the head like some dumb animal. I am quite keen on keeping my eye in by shooting vermin like jackal, hyena and zebra. But the real prize is one of the Big Five.

I am having some trouble finding an elephant gun. Not even my contacts on the Cape Flats have been able to help. Perhaps you could point me in the right direction. You will agree that if I am going to work my way through the Big Five, I will need a Big Gun. Anything that can drop an elephant is my kind of weapon. A black rhino in full charge would be child's play with hardware this powerful. Even a lion would be no match for me. As for the other two members of the Big Five, the cheetah and the hippo, I could probably beat them to death with the butt of the rifle.

I understand that canned hunting is gaining in popularity. This sounds like the one for me. I am not one of those hunters who likes to spend his day endlessly tracking spoor and sniffing dung to see how fresh it is. Give me a comfortable chair, an air-conditioned hide and a clear shot at anything that comes down to the waterhole. My neighbour tells me that as a member of the SA Hunters Association, I will get special rates at game farms that provide canned hunting. Will my membership include one of those waistcoats with pockets for your bullets and grenades? If not, I hope that I will at least get to learn a funny handshake so that I can identify fellow members out on the hunt.

Please let me know what it costs to become a lifetime member. And whether I can purchase an elephant gun through your organisation. Enclosed is a ten rand deposit.

Yours truly,

....
Ben Trovato (Mr)

S.A. Jagters- en Wildbewaringsvereniging
S.A. Hunters' and Game Conservation Association

Kamdeboweg 626 Kamdebo Rd
Florauna
0182

Tel: (012) 565-4856
Tel: (012) 546-2622
Tel: (012) 546-1636
Fax: (012) 565-4910
E-Mail: sahunt@mweb.co.za

Posbus/P.O. Box 18108
Pretoria-Noord/North
0116

27 August 2002

Dear Mr Trovato

Your letter dated 28 July 2002 refers.

The information you have been given by your neighbour is totally incorrect, and the S.A. Hunters' and Game Conservation Association does not support your views on hunting.

We are unable to help you in any of your requests and therefore return the R10 deposit which accompanied your letter.

Yours faithfully

André van Dyk
Communication Manager

CASH RETURNED

131

Mr Mervyn Merrington
Chief of Traffic Police
PO Box 7064
Roggebaai
8012

Mr Ben Trovato
PO Box 1117
Sea Point
8060

31 July, 2002

Dear Sir,

Perhaps you could explain why the city is suddenly crawling in policemen dressed from head to toe in black. Is this a neo-fascist revival? Is it Mussolini Awareness Month?

I always drive well below the speed limit, so you can imagine my surprise when I rounded a corner in Sea Point the other day to find the road full of men who looked as if they had been dressed by the House of il Duce. They would not let me pass. Instead, they directed me to a nearby parking lot where I was dragged from the car, pistol whipped and sodomised with cattle prods while a Maserati driver roared past with his freshly clipped moustache caked in prime Colombian cocaine.

I regained consciousness to find a man called Benito van der Spuy demanding to see my driver's licence. Obviously I never had it with me. You would have to be out of your mind to go out in public carrying anything of importance these days. Unless I am mistaken, the latest police statistics indicate that you have a one in three chance of being mugged in the city. The odds are lowered to one in five in the suburbs. You may have heard that there are Nigerian syndicates operating freely in Sea Point. Given half a chance, they will take your shoes, let alone your driver's licence.

I tried explaining this to the thug in black, but he quickly pressed the sharp edge of his boot against my throat and held me against the pavement until I agreed to stop resisting.

I find it hard to believe that the traffic department is actively encouraging motorists to carry valuable documents that will almost certainly bring death or serious injury to the bearer. Why, sir, are you encouraging the Nigerians? I must warn you that some of my friends are Italian partisans. And the next time I am stopped, things will be different.

More importantly, who is going to pay my R200 fine?

I need to hear from you soon.

Yours truly,

Ben Trovato (Mr)

PS. The streets will be empty of the Blackshirts within a few weeks. Please tell me what happens to them when they have finished victimising the city's motorists. Where do they go? Administration, I suppose, what with their talent for taking down names, addresses and one's trousers with the sole purpose of administering a rectal reprimand.

Paul Sauer
1 Adderley Street
P O Box 7586, Roggebaai 8012
Ask for: Mr. G. Bontempi
Tel: 021 400–1418
Fax: 021 400–1402
E-Mail: giovanni.bontempi@capetown.gov.za
URL: http://www.capetown.gov.za/
Ref: HO 6/10/5
Filename:

ePaul Sauer
1 Adderley Street
P O Box 7586, Roggebaai 8012
Cela: Mnu G. Bontempi
Umnxeba: 021 400–1418
Ifeksi: 021 400–1402
iE-Mail: giovanni.bontempi@capetown.gov.za
URL: http://www.capetown.gov.za/
Iref:

Paul Sauer
Adderleystraat 1
Posbus 7586, Roggebaai 8012
Vra vir: Mnr G. Bontempi
Tel: 021 400–1418
Faks: 021 400–1402
E-pos: giovanni.bontempi@capetown.gov.za
URL: http://www.capetown.gov.za/
Verw:

CITY OF CAPE TOWN
ISIXEKO SASEKAPA
STAD KAAPSTAD

CAPE TOWN ADMINISTRATION
Community Service
City Police

21 August 2002

Dear Sir

Your letter to Mr. Mervyn Merrington, dated 31 July 2002 refers.

Since 1989 it has been a requirement in terms of the Road Traffic Act (Act 29 of 1989) that all drivers carry their drivers licence and produce it on demand to a Police Official or Traffic Officer. This fact has been well documented and publicized. With regards to this specific incident, it is suggested that you wait for the relevant summons and approach the Courts directly.

Yours faithfully

G. BONTEMPI
DIVISIONAL COMMANDER
CAPE TOWN CITY POLICE

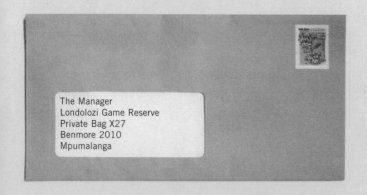

Mr Ben Trovato
PO Box 1117
Sea Point
8060
Cape Town
South Africa

1 August, 2002

Dear Sir,

My wife and I are planning a second honeymoon and we have always wanted to visit Londolozi. We have heard so much about the place, especially from our friends in the government.

We are hoping to spend two weeks at the lodge, and would need your finest suite towards the end of October.

I understand the weather is pleasant at that time of year. Let us know what we can expect, since I need to know what clothing to pack. My wife, on the other hand, will not be packing much. She is a nudist, you see. For years we used to go on outings and strip off together. But the harsh African sun took its toll on my poor willy, and the doctor advised that I cover up. So whenever Brenda wants to go au naturel, I slip into a skimpy pair of leopard skin briefs and my Johnson lives to fight another day.

Brenda is something of a purist in that her decisions on where and when to wear clothes are guided by the weather and not by social considerations. This means that on a balmy evening, Brenda may well choose to dine in the buff. We would not want to alarm the other guests, so you may want to allocate us a table in a discreet corner of the room.

Game drives could prove to be a little more awkward, but I assume that most of your guests will be more interested in trying to spot the Big Five than catch a glimpse of my Brenda's hamster. Unless they are German, of course. In which case I shall deploy my 250-volt Tazer. You need not worry about fatalities. Even a Pacemaker can withstand the shock. Most of the time. It is vital that a woman's dignity is protected, not so?

If I do not hear from you, please expect our arrival around the 15th of October.

Yours truly,

Ben Trovato (Mr)

PS. We are also practicing gymnosophists and will be performing our rituals in the privacy of our room. Unless, of course, our visit coincides with the full moon.

CC AFRICA

CONSERVATION CORPORATION AFRICA

2 September 2002

Dear Mr. Ben Trovato

We are in receipt of your letters to Ngala Private Reserve as well as Londolozi.

Unfortunately we do not believe that our operation is suitable for your specific needs.

Thank you
Yours Truly,
YVONNE SHORT
DIRECTOR SA LODGES

The Manager
Meikles Hotel
Cnr 3rd Street / Jason Moyo Avenue
Harare
Zimbabwe

Mr Ben Trovato
PO Box 1117
Sea Point
8060
South Africa

2 August, 2002

Dear Sir,

My wife and I are planning one last trip to Zimbabwe before the country goes up in flames. Our friends in the government tell us there is only one place in which to stay in Harare, and that is the Meikles. However, none of them have been there since President Mugabe lost his marbles and I was wondering if you had the same high standards of three or four years ago.

I would not wish to arrive at the Meikles only to find that the porters had been replaced by 14-year-old machete-wielding war veterans. I am a trained Signalman, so I know how to defend myself. But Brenda would not react terribly well to being rounded up at dawn and marched to breakfast at gunpoint.

I understand that most of the country has run out of food. Would you suggest that we bring along a hamper or have you got the Red Cross on your side? This is our second honeymoon and we would not want to sacrifice the Beluga, Moet and other essentials.

My neighbour tells me that tourists now have to check in with the Central Intelligence Organisation. Do you have a representative at the hotel, or would we have to go to their offices? Perhaps this applies only to homosexuals from Britain.

Unless you expect civil war to break out soon, please let me know if your finest suite will be available for two weeks towards the end of September.

Thank you.

Yours truly,

Ben Trovato (Mr)

MEIKLES

Zimbabwe's Premier Hotel

8 August 2002

Dear Mr Trovato

Thank you for your letter, your sense of humour has lightened an otherwise miserable Thursday morning.

I have booked the Imperial suite for the period 15th – 30th September 2002 and trust that you will find comfort in this little haven away from the anarchy that exists at the moment.

I would like to believe that despite the prevailing situation, you will find the Hotel standards intact and up to previously acceptable standards.

Please can you provide me with your flight details and exact dates so I can organize a military escort to collect you from the Harare "International" Airport.

We look forward to accommodating you at the Meikles Hotel and trust you will have a relaxing and "peaceful" stay.

Yours sincerely

KARL SNATER
GENERAL MANAGER

Mr Ben Trovato
PO Box 1117
Sea Point
8060

6 August, 2002

Dear Sir,

I wish to complain about Metrorail's decision to give "senior citizens" a whopping forty percent discount on their train fares. This is patently unfair. It is the younger generations who need the discounts. We still have a long time left to live and we need all the money we can get our hands on if we hope to make it to the end in one piece.

These so-called "senior citizens" are already pulling in to the last station on the line. It makes no difference to them if they pay the full fare, half fare or no fare at all. I do not want to sound callous, but they will be dead soon. They have little use for money.

Old people do not get around that much. You do not see them running to catch a train, nor do you see them hanging from the doors and windows of the first class carriages. Do you know why? Because they are at home twitching and burbling and watching re-runs of that dreadful Felicia. They are not catching the trains. Well, maybe a few are regular commuters. But then again, where would they be going? Certainly not to the lunchtime show at Teazers. Unlike your younger passengers who use the trains regularly for a variety of reasons.

Perhaps that is your strategy. Mount a high-profile advertising campaign telling everyone that senior citizens can now get tickets for nearly half the regular price. The subtext says that Metrorail cares about old people. The reality is that two half-blind grannies from Woodstock and an octogenarian from Elsies River are the only people who will benefit. This means that Metrorail suffers a revenue loss of R7,50 and gains the undying admiration of "Premier" Marthinus van Schalkwyk's puppet regime.

Even though the only time you would catch me on one of your trains is if I suffered a massive heart attack and a train happened to be going to Groote Schuur Hospital at that very moment, I am speaking for all the voiceless passengers who are being penalised for not having aged fast enough to make use of this exciting new offer.

Should an explanation and an apology not be forthcoming, I shall engage in rolling mass pickets at stations around the province. And I will not be alone.

Yours truly,

Ben Trovato (Mr)

PS. In view of latest developments, you may want to consider using the slogan: "Youth comes at a price".

15 August 2002

Dear Mr Trovato

COMPLAINT RE 'SENIOR CITIZEN'S' DISCOUNT

Your letter dated the 6th August 2002 refers.

Metrorail's policy is to be a socially responsible company and while living in Sea Point might not expose you to the serious plight of thousands of the elderly in the townships surrounding Cape Town, we as a company have taken a decision to assist in their mobility.

While Sea Point is relatively close to the city, many of our black citizens were moved further away during the apartheid era. This discount is aimed at giving them accessibility to other parts of the metropole.

I trust this resolves your concerns about Metrorail's decision.

Yours sincerely

ANDRÉ HARRISON
REGIONAL MANAGER

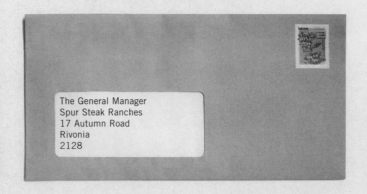

Mr Ben Trovato
PO Box 1117
Sea Point
8060

6 August, 2002

Dear Sir,

I would like to inform you that someone who claims to be a former high-ranking member of your team has been in touch with me. He is offering to sell me the recipe for Spur's secret sauce. At quite a price, I might add.

I run my own "burger 'n chips" outlet from a caravan outside my home. It may not sound like much competition to Spur, but I get an extraordinary amount of passing trade. There is no doubt in my mind that if I do purchase the recipe, it will only be a matter of time before I set up caravans around the country.

At the moment, my prices are lower than yours. And when I open up franchises using the secret formula on my burgers, I expect most of your customers will be quick to switch allegiances.

I assume you would want to avoid a situation that could well lead to Spur going out of business. If so, I am prepared to make a very generous offer. I am willing to sell the recipe back to you at double the price.

If you are interested, please let me know as soon as possible and we can talk numbers. If not, expect to see a "Sphur Burger™" caravan appearing on a street corner near you.

You have been warned.

Yours truly,

Ben Trovato (Mr)

12 August 2002

REF: DHL2706/as

Dear Mr Trovato

We refer to your letter dated 6th August with reference to Spur recipes. Please would you contact the writer on Telephone No. (021) 462-1293 or 082-444-4439.

Yours sincerely

pp A.E. Sinclair

DEAN HYDE
FINANCIAL DIRECTOR
For and on behalf of
SPUR GROUP (PTY) LTD

c.c. Pierre van Tonder

Mr Ben Trovato
PO Box 1117
Sea Point
8060

6 August, 2002

Dear Sir,

You are a difficult organisation to reach. I called your Customer Care Line to get your postal address and a woman told me that they are not allowed to give out this kind of information. What are you people afraid of? Complaints? Before you set the police on to me to find out how I got your address, let me just say that I picked up the telephone directory and there it was under Kentucky Fried Chicken.

The point of my letter is to inform you that someone who claims to be a former high-ranking member of your team has been in touch with me. He is offering to sell me the Colonel's secret recipe. At quite a price, I might add.

I run my own crunchy chicken outlet from a caravan outside my home. It may not sound like much competition to KFC, but I get an extraordinary amount of passing trade. There is no doubt in my mind that if I do purchase the secret recipe, it will only be a matter of time before I set up caravans around the country.

At the moment, my prices are lower than yours. In fact, my slogan is: "The Chicken That Goes Cheep". And when I open up franchises using the Colonel's formula, I expect most of your customers will be quick to switch allegiances.

I assume you would want to avoid a situation that could well lead to KFC going out of business. If so, I am prepared to make a very generous offer. I am willing to sell the recipe back to you at double the price.

If you are interested, please let me know as soon as possible and we can talk numbers. If not, expect to see a red and white Bentrovato Fried Chicken™ caravan appearing on a street corner near you.

You have been warned.

Yours truly,

Ben Trovato (Mr)

Restaurants International

26 August 2002

Dear Mr Trovato

USE OF KFC SECRET RECIPE

Your letter dated 6 August 2002 refers.

We note the contents of the above-mentioned letter and we hereby reserve all rights we may have at law. We further wish to advise you that we will fiercely oppose any attempted emulation of any of our products and will defend any infringement of our rights.

We are certain that you will take note of the above and will not act in any way that may be detrimental to you or your business.

Kind regards

LUIS BARRETO
LEGAL & FRANCHISING
TEL: (011) 540-1093
FAX: (011) 463-2160

CC: W Pretorius, B de Villiers

Mr Luis Barreto
Legal & Franchising
Tricon Restaurants International
PO Box 71105
Bryanston 2021

Mr Ben Trovato
PO Box 1117
Sea Point
8060

3 September, 2002

Dear Mr Barreto,

That is an Italian name, is it not? You may have noticed that I, too, am of the blood. My roots are in Sicily. And yours? Naples, probably, judging by the tone of your letter dated 26th August. You may have heard of Guido Trovato. If not, I am sure your relatives back home will recognise the name. Please be assured that this is not a threat. I am simply pointing out that I have friends in the family.

You say in your letter that you are certain I will not act in any way that may be detrimental to me or my business. Perhaps you are from Sicily, after all. These are tactics born in Palermo. However, a true Sicilian would have included my wife and children. And my elderly parents. And all my friends. And their friends. Neapolitans have never quite understood that retribution cannot be threatened in half measures.

Mr Barreto, I have good news for you. The recipe in my possession is not what I thought it was. My contact swore it was a copy of an extremely valuable document that was in the possession of no more than three of Kentucky Fried Chicken's most trusted managers. But when I got my wife to make up the secret concoction, it turned out to be nothing more than the glop used in the production of koeksusters. I was bitterly disappointed. And yet, at the same time, strangely relieved. To be honest, I was not looking forward to having you fiercely opposing me in court. We both know what happens when Italians begin hurling recriminations at one another in a confined space.

If you have already put your boys on me, please call them off immediately. It would be a terrible tragedy if I were to meet with an unfortunate "accident" when the issue has already been resolved.

I will not be going into competition against KFC and the Colonel's secret is safe. The crispy chicken market is all yours.

Omerta!

Ben Trovato

Mr Ben Trovato
PO Box 1117
Sea Point
8060

6 August, 2002

Dear Edith,

I hope you don't mind if I call you Edith. Ms Venter sounds so formal. Brenda and I have become so accustomed to seeing you on the social pages that we feel as if we almost know you!

I notice you have your own company dedicated to promoting yourself. Well, why not? Some celebrities pay other people, like that dreadful Brewster chap, a small fortune to get themselves into the papers and on to important guests lists. I am sure it is a lot cheaper to do it yourself. And there must be tax benefits, too.

We are planning a party in the next couple of weeks and Brenda suggested that we invite you. Between you and me, I suspect she is merely trying to impress Mary Goodfellow from across the road. Mary had a dinner party the other night and Brenda thought she spotted Allan Boesak walking up the driveway. The next day she confronted Mary and said she ought to be ashamed of herself. Mary quickly denied that it was Boesak, but a few days later she was unable to explain where all her good silver had disappeared to.

Anyway, the point is that we need a little glamour to liven up the proceedings. You are certainly one of the most refined women I have come across in a long time. It is hard to imagine that you were once married to a man capable of building such a hideous monstrosity on the Clifton hillside. With taste like that, I am not surprised you ditched him. Are you taken at the moment? Just curious. If you have a beau, it might be better if you left him at home when you come to our home. There is nothing that gets a soiree going quicker than a beautiful single woman who gives the appearance of not being quite sure who she will be taking home later in the evening.

To be honest, I would be surprised to hear that you accepted all of these invitations out of the good of your heart. Nobody can be that generous. After all, you are in the business of marketing yourself. It makes sense to charge for appearances. I am including a small cash deposit to secure your presence. Obviously there is much more where that came from.

Let us know how you are placed for the 24th of August.

Thank you so much.

Yours truly,

Ben Trovato (Mr)

Edith Venter Promotions

22 August 2002

Mr Ben Trovato
P.O. Box 1117
Sea Point
8060

Dear Ben

What a wonderful letter, dated 6th August, which you sent to me inviting me to dinner. It was a happy start to the day and I thank you for all your kind comments regarding me. I don't think I have ever been accused of stealing the silver or anything else for that matter !!!

I try to accommodate all invitations, especially charity related, as I know from my work with cancer how hard it is for charities to raise funds.

Unfortunately, I only received your letter on Monday and as you gave no telephone number, I was unable to contact you immediately to let you know that it would be impossible to be in Cape Town today.

The R10-00 is not necessary and I, therefore, return it to you and hope it becomes "lucky" money for you.

I do hope that we will have the pleasure of meeting with you and Brenda sometime when next I am in Cape Town. Once again, thank you for your very hilarious letter – it's the most unique invitation I have ever received.

Kind regards

EDITH VENTER

Enc.

Mr Ben Trovato
PO Box 1117
Sea Point
8060
Cape Town

6 August, 2002

Dear Sir,

As an expert in these matters, I am sure you will be able to assist me.

I am having problems with my dairy cow, Manto. I bought her fairly recently and she stays out on a plot of land I have near Betty's Bay. I visit her most weekends with a view to obtaining a few litres of milk. However, Manto refuses to give me anything. I tug and tug at her udders but not a drop comes out.

Clover has been producing milk ever since I was a little boy. What are you doing that I am not? Am I pulling incorrectly? Does Manto need to have the company of a bull before she makes milk? Is it possible that Manto is, in fact, a bull?

I am desperate. Every time I go to the plot, my wife hands me two plastic canisters to fill up. And every time I have to stop at a 7-11 on the way home, buy four litres of milk and empty them into the containers. Brenda is amazed at the quality of Manto's milk, and I dare not tell her the truth.

I would deeply appreciate any suggestions you may have.

Thank you.

Yours truly,

Ben Trovato (Mr)

The Production Manager
Clover SA
PO Box 6161
Weltevreden Park
Johannesburg

Mr Ben Trovato
PO Box 1117
Sea Point
8060
Cape Town

29 August, 2002

Dear Sir,

I wrote you on the 6th of August but have not yet had a reply.

If you recall, I was asking for a little advice on how to get milk from my cow. You may have gathered that I am not much of a farmer. However, Manto has large udders and it seems such a waste not to tap this rich resource. But as I mentioned, I have had no luck in getting her to part with even a single drop.

As someone who is an expert in the milk business, I was sure you would be able to assist me. I can only assume that your failure to respond is linked to my failure to provide the necessary incentive. Nothing, not even information, comes free these days. Enclosed please find ten rand to cover your costs.

I hope to hear from you very soon. Manto looks like she is about to burst.

Yours truly,

Ben Trovato (Mr)

MILK PROCUREMENT/MELKWINNING
Vry Street/straat, Heilbron 9650
PO Box/Posbus 750, Heilbron 9650
Tel: (058) 853-3341
Fax/Faks: (058) 853-3323
E-mail/E-pos: anduples@clover.co.za

NATIONAL CO-OPERATIVE DAIRIES LIMITED
NASIONALE SUIWELKOÖPERASIE BEPERK

Dear Ben,

Thank you for your letter stating the problem that you had with Manto. I tried to get hold of your telephone number to save time but apparently it is not listed. We apologise for the late response. Something must have happened to the first letter as we have no record of receiving it.

I assume that your problem with Manto started immediately after calving because this is common that lactating cows do not release milk after calving. Milk release in the udder is a physiological process controlled by the hormone oxitosine. After calving the cow is normally under stress and if circumstances in and around the parlour is such that the cow does not relax sufficiently the brain does not release enough of the hormone into the blood stream for the alveoli mussels in the udder to release the milk. If she does not release milk after the first two milkings you need to advise a vet. Normal treatment will be to inject the cow with oxitisine for two or three days. Usually the cow responds very rapidly to the treatment and should not have much of a problem thereafter. I am however concerned that in Manto's case it is very late to apply this kind of treatment and I presume that some complication to the udder might have stepped in. Please consult your vet immediately. A few practical tips:

1. If the cow had a difficult calving she will be under stress. Give her an injection of oxitosine.

2. Make sure that the calf had the opportunity for the first three days to suck from the udder. This will relax the cow and give the calf the opportunity to drink the colostrum that it needs.

3. Make sure that the milking process is relaxing to the cow. Do not hit or shout at her.

4. Give her something to eat while you milk her.

I do hope that this will solve your problem. Please find enclosed you R10 sent to us.

Kind regards

Marius Nel.

MARIUS NEL
Managing Director: Agri Services and Transport

Mr Ben Trovato
PO Box 1117
Sea Point
8060
Cape Town

9 September, 2002

Dear Mr Nel,

Thank you so much for replying to my enquiries regarding my cow, Manto.

I shall certainly take your advice and inject her with oxitosine. It sounds like just the stuff she needs to begin giving us buckets of milk.

The only problem is that my wife is recovering from a rather nasty drug addiction and it is probably not a good idea for me to leave syringes lying around the house. Knowing Brenda, she will inject herself as soon as I turn my back. I will certainly take every precaution to make sure this does not happen. But if I am distracted, by something good on the telly, for example, and she manages to get a few cubic centimetres of oxitosine into her system, I need to know if she will also begin producing milk. If this is the case, would you recommend that I refrain from hitting or shouting at her as well? How long would it be before our relationship could return to normal? I will make sure Brenda gets something to eat, but I cannot promise that I will be able to milk her. I may have to bring in a specialist for that.

Do not worry if you are unable to set my mind at rest on this score. It is probably best that I consult a doctor. Or maybe a vet.

Thank you again for all your help.

Ben Trovato (Mr)

Mr Ben Trovato
PO Box 1117
Sea Point
8060

7 August, 2002

Dear Sir,

I wrote to the Institute on 13th August, 2001, and have not yet received a reply

I am sure you are snowed under by the mail, but even politicians manage to write back within a year.

If you recall, I was enquiring about a road rage course that was being held in Bloemfontein.

What happened to my application?

More importantly, what happened to my ten rand that I sent as a deposit? Ignoring the public is one thing, but taking their hard earned cash is clearly another.

Do you intend having any more courses on aggressive driving? If not, please return my money.

Thank you.

....
Ben Trovato (Mr)

Mr Ben Trovato
PO Box 1117
Sea Point
8060

13 August, 2001

Dear Mr Grimbeek,

I understand the Institute is planning to hold a Road Rage and Aggressive Driving Symposium in Bloemfontein on October 15, and I would like to register as a delegate.

I have come close to death on many occasions while taking my car for a spin. They seem to lie in wait for me, then come lunging out of each driveway and side road that I pass. They box me in and cut me off at every opportunity. I get sworn at, spat on and vilified by everyone from truck drivers to little old ladies.

I now realise that the problem lies with me. I am a passive driver and I appear to incite people whenever I get behind the wheel. It has become clear that I must change if I hope to survive. This is why I was so pleased to hear about your symposium.

I am confident that the Institute is able to teach even the most placid motorist basic aggressive driving skills. I wouldn't want to start off with anything too fancy. Perhaps a little rush-hour lane switching without the use of indicators, and progressing until I reach the stage where I am comfortable with overtaking on a blind rise with a cellphone in one hand, a beer in the other and my knees gripping the steering wheel.

Blinding your opponent is clearly an important strategy that timid drivers like myself tend to overlook. However, I have invested in a pair of powerful halogen arc lights and plan on welding them to the roof racks.

On the road rage front, I presume that beginners get to start out with a crash course in hand signals and facial expressions. But I fear this will not be enough. I would like to know what you offer in the way of high-speed intimidation techniques. And it goes without saying that I will need to learn the art of hand-to-hand combat. I want to become one of those men who can have a driver out of his seat and face down on the asphalt within three seconds. Five, if the window is closed.

Enclosed please find ten rand as a deposit towards my registration fee. Looking forward to seeing you at the symposium!

Yours truly,

B Trovato
....
Ben Trovato (Mr)

BRIBE GIVEN R10

INSTITUTE OF TRAFFIC AND MUNICIPAL POLICE OFFICERS OF SOUTHERN AFRICA

Tel: (018) 297 6388
(018) 299 5490
Fax: (018) 297 6388

website: www.itmpo.org.za
e-mail: itmposa@xsinet.co.za
info@itmpo.org.za

Private Bag X 1258
POTCHEFSTROOM
2520

16 August 2002

Dear Sir

Could you please supply me with your physical residential address on receipt of which I will contact you.

Yours faithfully

THEO R GRIMBEEK
HONORARY SECRETARY

TRG/sr

153

Mr Ben Trovato
PO Box 1117
Sea Point
80607

25 August, 2002

Dear Mr Grimbeek,

I received your reply dated 16th August and, to be honest, I am alarmed that you want to find out where I live.

I hope I have not given you the impression that there is something more between us. I was writing to you purely in a professional capacity. If you are looking for company, I suggest you try the classified section of your local paper. Internet chat rooms are another way to meet people. Or so I have heard.

I have gone through both of my letters over and over again, and I am unable to find even a hidden suggestion that you and I get together at my place. This can only mean one thing. That you would like an altogether more serious word with me. Is it because I expressed an interest in brushing up on my aggressive driving tactics? It is unlikely that you wish to give me private lessons. This leaves only one conclusion. That the men from the Institute intend turning up at my front door with batons and electrified cattle prods to teach me how to be a model motorist.

Quite frankly, both scenarios scare me. Right now, all I want is my money back. I wish I had never heard of the ITMPO. The whole business is giving me sleepless nights and when I go out I keep thinking that I am being followed.

I am prepared to meet you, Mr Grimbeek. But on my terms. We must rendezvous at a public place such as a crowded restaurant or a busy shopping mall. My personal preference is the ice rink at Grandwest Casino. It is not important that you need to know how to skate. You can hire boots there. I will meet you in the middle of the rink at midday on the Sunday of your choice. Bring my money.

Yours truly,

Ben Trovato (Mr)

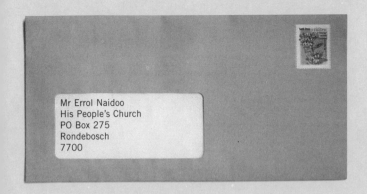

Mr Ben Trovato
PO Box 1117
Sea Point
8060

7 July, 2001

Dear Mr Naidoo,

As the spokesperson for His People's Church, I was alarmed to hear that you are busy promoting Cape Town as a destination for sex tourists.

May I remind you, Sir, of the state that cities like Bangkok find themselves in today. Beautiful young women offer themselves for a cupful of rice to total strangers who have to do nothing more than pay R5 750 for a return flight (four nights, breakfast included) to the city of original sin. That is if they fly from Johannesburg.

Apart from encouraging drug trafficking, racketeering, prostitution and disease, it will also encourage the Germans. And we both know what happens next. Sure, it starts with Klaus and Barbie arriving at the international airport wearing lederhosen and a brace of Hasselblads. But the next time you step outside to chase away the Jehovah's Witnesses, there is a Sherman tank parked in your driveway. Poland tried to introduce sex tourism in the 1940s, and look what happened there.

I implore you to rethink your stance. Right now, you may believe that encouraging sex tourism will create the impression of Cape Town being a "hip and happening" kind of place. "Phat", in the lingo of the drug-taking youth. Yes, the availability of good, cheap sex will result in many happy faces wandering around the streets of the city. But we have to look behind the smiles, beyond the ringing of the cash registers.

Even though you represent the People's Church, one must always bear in mind that the people are like sheep. And if you lie down with a lamb, you should be sent to jail.

I await your assurance that you will reconsider your position, as fashionable as it may be in these dangerously liberal times.

Yours truly,

Ben Trovato (Mr)

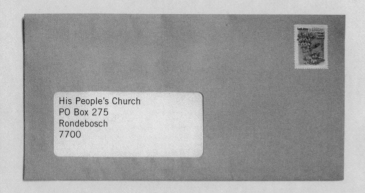

Mr Ben Trovato
PO Box 1117
Sea Point
8060

7 August, 2002

Dear Sir,

I wrote to the Church a year ago and have not yet received a reply. I am sure you must be swamped with mail from people wanting all sorts of things. But just in case it slipped through the cracks, I will refresh your memory.

There are several "respectable" organisations that support the positioning of Cape Town as a destination for sex tourists. I need to know if His People's Church is among them.

I am about to launch a campaign to rid the Mother City of sodomites and nymphomaniacs.

Are you with me or against me?

Let me know soon.

Yours truly,

....
Ben Trovato (Mr)

HIS PEOPLE
CHRISTIAN CHURCH

19 August 2002

Dear Mr. Trovato,

Firstly let me apologise for not replying to your previous letter. I must have misplaced it. I think there must have been some miscommunication regarding His Peoples stance on sex tourism. As a church we have been at the forefront of a number of battles regarding this issue.

We very definitely do not condone or encourage sex tourism of any kind. In fact, I personally was attacked in the media for challenging Cape Town Tourism for promoting our city as the "gay" capital of the world. We also led a protest at the unicity earlier this year against any promotion of Cape Town as a sex tourist destination.

There are, however, certain individuals in public office who are using their positions to promote this agenda. We will strive to be constantly vigilant with regard to this issue in the interest of our women and children.

Yours sincerely,

Errol Naidoo
Public Relations
His People Christian Church

Mr Ben Trovato
PO Box 1117
Sea Point
8060
Cape Town

7 August, 2002

The Managing Director
PROMEAL
PO Box 1558
Dassenberg
7350

Dear Sir,

I am writing to you in connection with a product of yours called 'Petley's'.

Last night, my wife broke a long-standing decision not to ever cook dinner for me again. Her reasons are not important. What is important is that, for the first time in ages, I could look forward to something other than a ham and cheese sandwich at supper time.

As if that wasn't enough, Brenda offered me a choice. I could either have the beef goulash or pilchard chunks in prawn flavoured jelly. I could not believe my luck! After embarrassing myself by begging to try a little of everything, Brenda disappeared into the kitchen and I dimmed the lights, poured the wine and put on the Barry White.

The meal was absolutely fantastic. The beef was tender and smothered in a tasty sauce. The pilchard chunks melted in my mouth, but to be honest I struggled to detect prawn in the jelly. But that's the only complaint I had. Until I went into the kitchen this morning.

I was emptying the bin when I noticed the cans from the night before. It was the pictures on the labels that caught my attention. One was of a spaniel. The other showed a fat, white Persian cat. I was curious to find out why any company would put animals on cans containing such fine food. The labels said: *'By appointment – Petley's Gourmet Supreme'*. Well and good. It certainly tasted like a gourmet meal. And Fortnum and Mason's products also bear the standard *'By Appointment'*, only in their case it is to Her Majesty the Queen. Above the spaniel's head it reads *'Beef Goulash Dinner'*. Since it was still repeating on me, I could confirm that. Next to the dog's left ear appear the words *'New Improved Recipe'*. That made sense. If Brenda had been following one of her old recipes, I would be having my stomach pumped right now. The tin that contained the pilchard chunks in prawn flavoured jelly was virtually identical, except there was a Persian in the spaniel's place. I assumed that your company is owned by an animal-lover and was about to take the garbage out when I noticed something else. The tin that once contained my seafood starter was covered in tiny cat shapes. The price tag caught my eye, too. Under four rand for a tin of such fine food? My suspicions were aroused.

Well, sir. You can imagine my reaction when I put on my bifocals and read the small print. I had just eaten a natural and well balanced meal meant for my dog. And my cat. And I had asked for seconds. With mounting horror, I read the ingredients. My hors d' oeuvre, which had me licking my plate, contained crude protein, crude fat, crude fibre and crude ash. Crude ash? Who the hell eats ash?

Appaled at what I had consumed, I studied the ingredients in my beef goulash hoping to find something vaguely suitable for human consumption. No such luck. In fact, in addition to the crude ingredients was a 2.2 min of phosphorus. Dear God. I was in the army and I know the damage a phosphorus grenade can do. Now I dare not leave the house for fear of turning into a blinding white fireball while out buying the morning paper.

It turns out that four percent of my prawn flavoured starter contained real pilchards. The rest is made up of 'fish derivatives'. When I see snoek fisherman ripping open the bellies of their catch and dragging out red and yellow and purple strands of glutinous gunk, are they removing the derivatives? It gets worse. Twenty-six percent of my goulash was made from beef. That's right. A one in four chance of hitting real meat. The other 74% of my main course was "animal derivatives". Let us not even speak of this.

Then I found the instructions. "Feed adult cats at least twice daily, serving as much Petley's as they will eat." This explains why the Persian on the label looks like a hairy beachball with eyes. It also says that lactating cats may require up to four times as much as normal adults. This is just what my home needs. A giant fur-covered animal armed with razor-sharp teeth and claws experiencing violent mood swings and leaking milk from six breasts while it buries its snout in a bottomless mound of pilchard chunks in prawn flavoured jelly. Christ. Not even Odysseus came across anything remotely like this on his way back to Ithaca.

As for the spaniel with the blow-dried ears, he appears to fall into the Medium Dog category that apparently should be given up to half a kilogram of beef goulash at one sitting. I have seen fully-grown pensioners get by on 500g of goulash a week. But I suppose the spaniel saves on clothing and transport costs. When Brenda made me dinner, she obviously never consulted the feeding guide. Otherwise she would have seen that Large Dogs should be given up to 1,7kgs of Petley's Gourmet Supreme at least once a day. It is this kind of feeding that turns small dogs into very big ones. Unlike cats, dogs do not stop eating when they are full. Given unlimited access to Petley's beef goulash, a daschund could easily grow into something quite capable of pulling a sled on the Iditarod Trail.

To be honest, I am conflicted. As I have said, last night's dinner was fabulous. But at the same time, I am nauseated. However, I cannot blame your company. That leaves Brenda. I thought of disciplining her, but that would certainly mean the end of any future dinners. My instincts tell me to keep quiet and continue complimenting Brenda on her fine beef goulash and seafood starters. I do, however, need vital information from you. How long can a man eat Petley's without a) manifesting pet-like characteristics and b) dying.

Please let me know soon.

Yours truly,

....
Ben Trovato (Mr)

Mr Ben Trovato
PO Box 1117
Sea Point
8060
Cape Town

29 August, 2002

Dear Sir,

I wrote to you on the 7th of August but have not yet had a reply. I am sure your letter has gone missing in the mail, since it is unlikely that you would ignore somebody who has grown to love your products.

In my previous correspondence, I expressed my appreciation for Petley's Gourmet Supreme range. However, I was also seeking assurances that it is safe to continue eating these products.

Another thing I would like to know is if you are considering bringing out chicken flavoured Petley's. The beef and pilchard chunks are delicious, but chicken would provide just that much more variety in my diet.

I appreciate that information does not come for free these days, so I am enclosing ten rand to cover your costs.

I would appreciate answers to my questions as soon as possible.

Yours truly,

....
Ben Trovato (Mr)

PROMEAL

PRODUCERS OF FINE CANNED PETFOODS
(PTY) LTD

Reg. No. 61/01324/07

03 September 2002

Dear Ben

Thank you for your humoristic letter of the 7th August 2002. We at the office really enjoyed it, so did our friends and family.

Should you wish so, we would like to deliver at your street address a free sample of our Petleys dogfood. Please let us know what your street address is. I would also like to know what your telephone number is to enable me to speak to you personally.

With reference to your letter of the 20th August 2002. We all know that this is a cut throat business, but if you want to send us a donation for survival, please make it worthwhile (at least R100.00).

Looking forward to hear from you.

Yours sincerely

....
Mr. Gert Tolken
Managing Director
Promeal (Pty) Ltd

The Managing Director
Reckitt Benckiser
8 Jet Park Road
Elandsfontein
1406

Mr Ben Trovato
PO Box 1117
Sea Point
8060

8 August, 2002

Dear Sir,

When I first met my wife many years ago, I did not have many possessions. In fact, I had little more than the clothes on my back. At the time, there was another fellow who was competing with me for Brenda's favours. In those days, one of her favours could leave you with a smile on your face for two weeks. My rival suitor came from a wealthy Afrikaans family, and he used to try to convince Brenda that he was a far better prospect since he had *"baie geld"* and I had *"min geld"*.

This appealed to Brenda's warped sense of humour and she immediately began referring to me as Mr Min. I won't bore you with the details, but suffice it to say that I got the girl.

It has not escaped my notice that one of your products is called Mr Min. It is obvious where the name comes from. Binky van der Spuy gave it to you. He was devastated when Brenda chose me over him. And this is how he got his revenge. To those who knew me, the name Mr Min always conjured up romantic images of an impoverished poet struggling for his art. Now it conjures up images of furniture polish.

I think you will agree that I am owed some sort of compensation for the use of my name over the years.

I will leave it up to you to decide what you think is fair.

Without justice there can be no peace.

Yours truly,

....
Ben Trovato (Mr)

RECKITT BENCKISER

21 August 2002

Dear Mr Trovato

I am very happy that, despite you had *min geld*, Brenda made a wise decision and chose you.

Of course your request of Compensation has no basis and cannot be satisfied, but I would like you to have a full sample line up of your favourite Mr. Min brand, so that you can think of and remember your past successes. Just one question: do you still enjoy Brenda's favours and, if so, do they still leave you with a smile for two weeks?

Thanks for your support to Mr. Min brand, which can be considered as one of the historical consumer values in South Africa.

Yours sincerely

Salvatore Caizzone
Senior Vice President, Regional Director – Africa & Middle East

The International Missionary
Association
PO Box 74169
Turffontein
Johannesburg

Mr Ben Trovato
PO Box 1117
Sea Point
8060

13 August, 2002

Dear Sir,

I have reached a stage where I need to do something that will make me feel as if my life has been worth something. The odds are heavily against cracking the big one on the Dream Machine at GrandWest, so I thought the next best thing would be to convert people to Christianity. At least there is a guaranteed return.

Are there any heathen savages left in the world? While I am prepared to travel, it would be nice to do the Lord's work a little closer to home. I was thinking of the North Coast, between Umhlanga Rocks and Richards Bay. Have all the Zulus been done? If not, I am quite prepared to go out there and turn them into God-fearing, church-going people.

Saving souls must be a very rewarding occupation. I imagine you would need to be quite fit, too. From what I have heard, pagans can put up quite a fight. And when they resist the Word, I suppose one has to take action. At times like this, being a missionary must be physically draining. Heretics are dangerous people. And even more so if they have a broken bottle or an assegai in their hand.

It is a worthy challenge to turn agnostics into believers. I, myself, am married to a woman who is a doubter. She rarely believes anything I say. But I have been practicing my technique on her and I think she is beginning to see the light. Or she will when the bandages come off, at any rate.

Please let me know what I have to do to qualify as a missionary. I would also need some sort of handbook that could serve as a guide in tough situations. For example, Reverend Allan Boesak is a Christian. Then he went to jail for theft and fraud. And when he came out he was still bleating about being a sacrificial lamb, so it's my guess that he needs some kind of redemption. What would be the missionary's position in a case like this?

I need to get started as soon as possible. In fact, I have already turned my neighbour into a Protestant. He was a Catholic. Are missionaries allowed to do inter-denominational conversions? No matter. I can stick with the sun worshippers for now.

I look forward to hearing from you.

Yours in Christ

Ben Trovato (Mr)

PS. I assume the association provides newcomers with protective clothing and weapons. If not, I can borrow something from my wife. Let me know. Here's R10 in case.

INTERNATIONAL MISSIONARY SOCIETY
SEVENTH DAY ADVENTIST REFORM MOVEMENT
Southern African Union – Reg. No.: 017-270 NPO

98 BERTHA STREET- TURFFONTEIN 2140- SOUTH AFRICA
P. O. BOX 74169. TURFFONTEIN 2140. SOUTH AFRICA
TELEPHONE (27) 011- 683 5406. FAX (27) 011-683 5406 E-MAIL info@imssdarm-sau.org.za

20 August 2002

Dear Mr Trovato

Re: Qualification of being a missionary

May the peace of God be unto you.

Thank you for your letter dated 13th August 2002. It is very much encouraging to know that the Lord still has many *'who have not bowed the knee to the image of Baal'* and are willing to enter the vineyard of the Lord.

Every one has been called to be a co-worker with Christ in the work of soul saving. However Christ has said in Mathew 28:20 *"Teaching them to observe all things whatsoever I have commanded you:.* Therefore before one could be sent out as a missionary, he has to be instructed in the Biblical truths (not indoctrinated) so that we may all come to the unity of faith. There after he could be sent to the field just like the disciples who were trained by Christ before receiving the commission.

Therefore in your case I would advise and suggest that we first have Bible instructions with you by someone in Cape Town and we take it from there.

I hope my advice will meet your favorable consideration. Any queries please direct them to me. Once again thank you for showing interest to enter into the Lord's vineyard.

Yours in Christ

Elijah Zwane

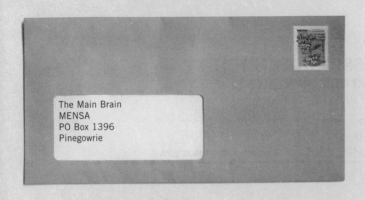

Mr Ben Trovato
PO Box 1117
Sea Point
8060

15 August, 2002

Dear Sir,

I think you would be interested in having my boy, Clive, as a member of your fine organisation.

He is very smart and may well be a genius. Although he is not much good with numbers, Clive possesses the uncanny ability to turn the most innocuous object into an incendiary device. The other day he spent a couple of hours fiddling with an ordinary toaster. Then he called my wife and I into the garden for the most remarkable demonstration. At the push of a button, the toaster became airborne, circled the house twice and then shot straight up into the air where it exploded. Luckily the shrapnel dispersed over a wide area. Clive says his invention will change the face of urban warfare.

I am enclosing R10 towards his membership fee. As soon as Clive receives his free cap and T-shirt, I will send the rest.

Yours truly,

Ben Trovato (Mr)

PS. My wife, Brenda, says your name is sexist. She wants to know why you don't get with the times and drop the MEN part of your name. Knowing her, she won't rest until she gets a satisfactory response.

MENSA SOUTH AFRICA

29 August 2002

Dear Mr Trovato

Thanks for your letter, and the R10. I am returning it for you to use for a Mensa test for your son. I will contribute to the test fee.

Interesting invention, I am sure it will find application somewhere.

As for the sexist name of Mensa, it has nothing to do with men and we have no intention of changing it to Peoplesa. It is Latin for table, and you will know that the French for table is la table – feminine, I hope that reassures your wife.

Regards

Tim Knights
National Chairman

NEDBANK
A division of Nedcor Bank Limited
'n Afdeling van Nedcor Bank Beperk

198-40

Date
Datum 29 Aug 2002
dd · mm · yyyy / jjjj

RANDBURG

Pay
Betaal   Ben Trovato   or bearer
                                                of toonder

Amount
Bedrag   ten Rands

                              R10-00

Returned Fee.   FOR MENSA SOUTH AFRICA

"0376 ":198405": 1984 429124" 04

Mr Ben Trovato
PO Box 1117
Sea Point
8060

17 August, 2002

Dear Sir,

I was on the point of approaching Santam to take care of my short-term insurance when I happened to read in the paper that the company has been listed as a gay-bashing organisation run by homophobic bigots.

To be honest, I generally have nothing against normal, red-blooded people who are driven to violence at the sight of men kissing one another. I have often felt the urge myself. To commit violence, I mean, not to kiss another man. In fact, this is one of the reasons I need insurance.

However, I am worried that the company is going to be severely affected as a result of the 'pinklisting' by that unholy bunch of catamites and coprophiliacs who go by the name of the Gay and Lesbian Alliance.

What guarantees are there that Santam will survive this unholy onslaught? I understand these lost souls are everywhere, not just Cape Town. A global uprising of left-handed nancy boys and bull dykes with motorcycle chains could well put you out of business.
The share price would be the first thing to go. Then your offices would be invaded by bands of gilded deviants scaring the staff with Sapphic war chants and engaging in tribadism right there on the boardroom table.

I thought of taking my business to Mutual & Federal until I saw that they, too, had been 'pinklisted'. What are we meant to do? Find a company run by screaming queers flouncing about in spandex bodysuits? Insurance is a tough game run by tough people. Directors are expected to show profits, not swan about in togas having shiatsu massages and burning rose scented incense in color-coded, feng shui aligned offices.

Please let me know if you think it is safe to invest in Santam.

Keep the faith.

Yours truly,

Ben Trovato (Mr)

PS. I see that if you admit guilt, apologise to the gay community and pay R20 000, your name will be taken off the pinklist. Enclosed please find R10 towards the fine.

Ons dek Suid-Afrika · Covering South Africa

21 August 2002

Dear Mr Trovato

Thank you for your letter that we received this morning.

The recent publicity that followed the actions taken by the Gay end Lesbian Alliance could possibly have created misconception and incorrect perceptions about Santam. I want to emphasise that we at Santam oppose any form of discrimination. We have responded to the GLA's accusations with a statement published on our website and in a general media release. I include a copy for your attention.

I can assure you that you do not have to worry in the least about entrusting us with you insurance matters. In the past eight decades we have proved over and again our ability to weather storms – of both the real kind and those brewing in teacups.

Thank you also for your kind contribution towards the imposed fine. We accept it with grace and have paid it over to the Santam Child Art Trust, an initiative enabling children in marginalized and previously disadvantaged communities to experience the joys of art classes.

Please feel free to contact our call centre on 0800 123 747 to discuss your insurance needs.

Yours sincerely

Steve Zielsman
Executive Head: Marketing

Mr Ben Trovato
PO Box 1117
Sea Point
8060

17 August, 2002

Dear Mr van Schalkwyk,

I was appaled to hear that you have been 'pinklisted' by the Gay and Lesbian Alliance as an intolerant, homophobic bigot. This certainly does not sound like the most powerful man in the country's best-run province!

What have you done to make the moffies so angry? I have not heard you make any statements that could remotely be construed as homophobic. I can only imagine that you were approached by one of them and rebuffed his advances. These people are very sensitive to rejection. But I have found that you cannot be gentle when turning them away. They are quick to sense weakness and they will bring you down like a pack of hyenas bring down a young springbok. I would suggest that you stay away from public urinals and move with a crowd. If you are isolated they will pick you off.

I suspect that they are aligning you with the National Party of old. In their minds, you still represent a regime that made sodomy illegal. They do not care that the same regime made it illegal to be black. All they care about is their right to fondle each other's buttocks. But it goes beyond that. They also want the right to fondle any buttocks that happen to come along. They believe that buttock fondling is a basic human right. Turn them down and they are quick to flounce off to the Constitution Court to claim in shrill voices that it is their bottoms they want violated, not their rights.

I find it ironic that they are targeting politicians who live in Cape Town, a city that has more tailgunners per square metre than the bathhouses of San Francisco. In Cape Town, it is easier to find a woman who has had a strapadicktomy than it is to find one who has had a hysterectomy.

They are hardly persecuted. In fact, they have their own bars, clubs, clothing stores and genetically modified vegetables. If anyone is oppressed, it is people like you and me. We are the minority here. Not them.

I understand that if you admit guilt, apologise to the bandits and hand over R5 000 to the Gay and Lesbian Alliance, your name will be removed from the pinklist. It seems that we either arm ourselves and go to war, or pay up. My weapon is oiled and ready. However, should you choose to take the soft option, I enclose ten rand towards your fine.

Keep up the good work and watch your backside!

Yours truly,

Ben Trovato (Mr)

Kantoor van die Premier
Office of the Premier
I-ofisi yeNkulumbuso

26 August 2002

Dear Mr Trovato

By direction of Mr MCJ van Schalkwyk, Premier of the Western Cape, I acknowledge receipt of your letter dated 17 August 2002, the contents of which have been noted.

Your R10.00 is hereby returned because it cannot be accepted.

Yours faithfully

CI NASSON
ADMINISTRATIVE SECRETARY

Mr Ben Trovato
PO Box 1117
Sea Point
8060

18 August, 2002

Dear Mr Baxter,

I understand you are in the process of 'naming and shaming' people and organisations that you consider to be homophobic. And that you charge R100 to have them blacklisted, or, as you put it, "pinklisted". I see your list already includes Mutual & Federal, Santam, the Dutch Reformed Church, the Apostolic Faith Mission, PW Botha, FW de Klerk, Marthinus van Schalkwyk and Peter Marais. You are even calling for a global tourism boycott of countries like Namibia and Zimbabwe.

I am deeply concerned that someone is going to give you my name. I am ashamed to admit that I used to live in Namibia. I also voted for FW de Klerk on two separate occasions and several years ago I attended a wedding in a Dutch Reformed Church. And I have an insurance policy with Mutual & Federal. To make matters even worse, I once called a woman a poisonous bull dyke because she refused to give up the pool table. However, I paid the price almost immediately when I was set upon by a mob of depraved cue-wielding faggots representing at least three genders.

I bitterly regret my actions and offer my wholehearted apologies. Please do not put me on your pinklist as I have a family and a reputation to protect.

However, my neighbour, Ted Goodfellow, is an appalling homophobe. When he goes out he thinks every second man is giving him the eye. By the end of the evening, he is convinced that absolutely everyone who is not a woman is trying to get at his bum. He has even taken to wearing a cricket box in case a gentleman brushes up against him at the bar and "accidentally" fondles his willy. I have tried telling him he is being paranoid. Then again, this is Cape Town we are talking about. Anything is possible.

I think Ted should be pinklisted for his own good. Nobody in their right mind would want their name linked to Peter Marais. I have no doubt he will come to his senses. I am unable to pay the full R100 to get him on to the list. Ten rand is all I can afford right now.

I understand that individuals must first admit guilt, publicly apologise to the gay community and pay R5 000 to get their names removed. I can assure you that Ted will cough up. So even though I am R90 short, you certainly gain in the long run.

Yours truly,

Ben Trovato (Mr)

PS. Any chance of a commission if I give you more names?

GAY & LESBIAN ALLIANCE
Lesbigay political voice of South Africa

26 August 2002

Sir,

The GAY & LESBIAN ALLIANCE (GLA), political voice of lesbigay South Africa acknowledges your letter dated 2002-08-18, regarding a homophobic individual in Cape Town.

We further acknowledge the amount of R10 as administration fee, thus we need the balance of R90 to ensure effective investigation and pinklisting.

Please forward or deposit the R90 balance, together with any form of contact details of the accused. Your identity will never be revealed to anyone. We also keep you inform through out our investigation. The period of investigation is a maximum of fourteen (14) days.

We hope to receive the above as a matter of urgency, to enable us to launch such a investigation.

Your Sincerely,

On behalf of the National Executive Board, GLA
Spokesperson DISCRIMINATION, RACISM & HOMOPHOBIC affairs.
Apuis Mokamedi

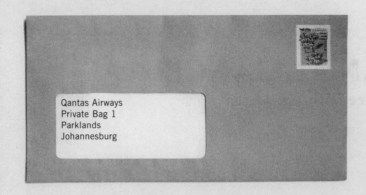

Mr Ben Trovato
PO Box 1117
Sea Point
8060

22 August, 2002

Dear Sir,

My wife and I are planning a trip to Australia and friends in the government have recommended that we fly Qantas.

However, I read in the paper recently that the Hollywood actor, John Travolta, was now working as a pilot for Qantas. To be honest, we would not feel safe with this man at the controls. For a start, he is a Scientologist and there is no telling what might happen when he is fifty thousand feet closer to whatever god it is these people worship.

Brenda says she seems to think that these cultists believe in aliens. She wants to know what would happen if Travolta suddenly decided to return to Zargon or wherever L Ron Hubbard originally comes from. Is the airline covered for this kind of eventuality?

If you can assure us that Travolta will not be at the helm, then we are in the market for a couple of first class tickets.

Please let us know soon as we need to make those bookings or find another airline that does not hire disco dancing thespians on a quest to fill their spiritual potential at the expense of ordinary travellers like Brenda and myself.

Thank you.

Yours truly,

Ben Trovato (Mr)

QANTAS

30th August 2002

Dear Mr Trovato

Thank you for your letter dated 22 August 2002 about actor John Travolta.

Mr Travolta has been employed by Qantas as an Ambassador. In this capacity he will be be operating any commercial flights.

Thank you for taking the time to write to us.

Yours sincerely

MICHAEL ADAMS
MANAGER AFRICA

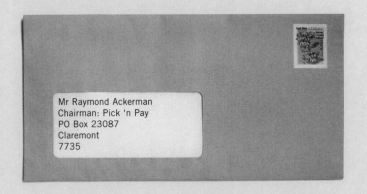

Mr Ben Trovato
PO Box 1117
Sea Point
8060

22 August, 2002

Dear Mr Ackerman,

Congratulations on writing such a fine book. It has inspired me to write to you with an idea that is bound to make you even more money.

The other day I overheard snippets of a radio discussion about hunting, I think it was, and someone said something about canned lions. What a splendid idea, I thought. I am not much of a chef, but I suspect that chunks of lion in a rich gravy would be delicious with a serving of Spanish rice and a small French salad.

Is it possible that you are already aware of this new product? If so, when can I expect to see it on your shelves? I am sure Proudly South Africa would like to be associated with a local product that is bound to be highly nutritious and full of protein. And tins of canned lion have more of an African flavour than tins of canned asparagus, for example.

Your advertising could say that it "Roars With Flavour". No, hang on. I think Simba has that slogan. But even if they do, I am fairly certain that their product contains synthetic lion. What about something like "The Beef with Teeth"? Just don't try saying it quickly over and over again. Or maybe "King of the Stews". Mind you, this is bound to incite the religious fundamentalists. What about giving your kids "The Lion's Share". And why not make lunch your "Mane" meal? You get the picture.

I have a lion suit which I wore during my honeymoon, and you might want to give some thought to the idea of hiring me to promote the new product at some of your stores in the Western Cape. The suit took a bit of a hammering but I think most of the stains will come out in the wash. It has also developed a patch of mange on the rump.

In the event that others have had the same idea, I am enclosing ten rand to help your secretary slip my name to the top of the list.

Yours truly,

....
Ben Trovato (Mr)

STORES LIMITED

28 August 2002

Dear Mr Trovato

Thank you for your letter and kind comments concerning my book – I am pleased you enjoyed it.

I appreciate your sense of humour, Mr Trovato ! and not only will the R10.00 you sent me, put you on "top of the list" as you say, but it will also help to swell the coffers of the "House for AIDS Orphans" charity.

With kind regards.

Yours sincerely

RAYMOND ACKERMAN

Dr Isak Burger
President: Apostolic Faith
Mission of South Africa
PO Box 890197
Lyndhurst 2106

Mr Ben Trovato
PO Box 1117
Sea Point
8060
Cape Town

5 August, 2002

Dear Dr Burger,

As a fellow Christian, I am sure you will agree with me when I say that advertising has become the Devil's trade. I am not talking about a housewife selling Skip, although some of these certainly do push the limits. I am talking about the amount of sex that is being used to sell certain products. Not only sex, but drugs too. Did you know that Sasol has an advert that encourages youngsters to get high with a little help from their friends?

But the adverts that really get my blood boiling are those for Magnum ice cream. I am not sure if you have seen them, but they border on the pornographic. I have done a little research and discovered that Unilever makes this particular product. I was appaled to learn that the company publicly, and proudly, admits that this is the "first ice cream developed especially for adults".

This obviously accounts for the lurid advertisements, one of which has a young woman moaning as if in the throes of sexual pleasure. Another caresses the ice cream with her tongue, implying that if you buy this product you will be surrounded by beautiful women wanting to lick your "ice cream" too.

What kind of degenerate perverts are these people? I would not be surprised to hear that advertising executives meet secretly in covens where they drink the blood of junior copywriters and carve pentagrams into one another's naked buttocks.

Encouraging young people to indulge in adult ice creams is where it all begins. The next thing you know, they are having unprotected sex in our restaurants and on our beaches. We live in an age of unbridled licentiousness and it is up to people like you and I to put a stop to it.

Please let me know what I can do to fight not only Unilever, but also every company that exploits men, women and animals as sexual objects to sell their products.

I enclose ten rand towards the war on smut.

Yours in Jesus Christ.

Ben Trovato (Mr)

The Apostolic Faith Mission Of South Africa

P.O. Box 890197, Lyndhurst, 2106
Tel: (011) 786-8550

Die Apostoliese Geloof Sending van Suid-Afrika

Posbus 890197, Lyndhurst, 2106
Tel: (011) 786-8550

From the desk of the President...
Van die lessenaar van die President...

9 September 2002

Dear Mr Trovato

Warm Christian greetings!

Thank you for your letter. I did receive your first letter as well as the ten rand. Thank you for the donation.

Magnum announced that they are withdrawing their planned advertisement due to the many objections. They are indeed planning a new ad which they say would exclude the words "seven deadly sins". As the new format is still a secret, I cannot comment on it. I've warned them that we will continue with our action if it is still offensive. Keep your eye on the press for more details.

Thank you for your support. I sincerely appreciate it!

Yours sincerely

DR ISAK BURGER

Mr Ben Trovato
PO Box 1117
Sea Point
8060

22 August, 2002

Dear Sir,

I have seen your latest advertising campaign. I am talking about the one where you use a little deaf girl to sell your product.

After giving it some thought, I came up with an idea for your next campaign. A little blind boy is walking along the pavement when he is suddenly hit in the face by a flying chicken. It might be best to use a rubber chicken since a real one could cause some damage with its claws and beak. This would get a huge laugh, I assure you. Here are some suggestions for the payoff line:

• "KFC - for people who would rather eat chicken than duck."
• "You might be blind – but our chicken isn't."
• "KFC - You don't have to see it to like it."
• "KFC...the low-frying chicken."
• "Nando's is for people who haven't heard about KFC."

I have more ideas using mute orphans and even amputees.

I am enclosing ten rand as a deposit on securing the advertising contract.

Let's make money!

Yours truly,

Ben Trovato (Mr)

Yum! *Restaurants International*

Restaurant Support Centre - Southern Africa

Yum! Restaurants International (Pty) Limited

Charlton House, Hampton Park

20 Georgian Cresent

Bryanston

P.O. Box 71105,

Bryanston 2021

South Africa

Tel: +27 (011) 540-1000

Fax: +27 (011) 463-2735

11 September 2002

Dear Mr Trovato

SUGGESTED MARKETING CAMPAIGN

Your letter dated 22 August 2002 refers, the contents thereof having been noted.

Our marketing strategies are formulated at a national and international level, utilizing the services of internal expert employees and external consultants. The services of these experts are used in conjunction with national and international market trends and market research information, and together serve to dictate current and future marketing and sales strategies.

Although your suggestions make for interesting reading, we do not believe that they are relevant to our current and future marketing strategies. However, should similar marketing mechanisms be implemented in the future, this will be as a result of an actual need in the market and not as a result of your suggestions. We record that we will not be forwarding your letter to our national and international marketing and sales departments, nor are we prepared to offer you any payment, now or in the future with regard to the suggestion set out in your letter.

We return herewith you R10,00 as received with your letter.

Kind regards

LUIS BARRETO

LEGAL & FRANCHISING

TEL: (011) 540-1093

FAX: (011) 463-2160

CC: W Pretorius, B de Villiers, M Willows

Mr Ben Trovato
PO Box 1117
Sea Point
8060

8 August, 2002

Governor Tito Mboweni
South African Reserve Bank
PO Box 427
Pretoria
0001

Dear Mr Mboweni,

Congratulations on the fine job that you are doing. It is not your fault that none of us can afford to go abroad on holiday. In the bad old days of apartheid the rand was a lot stronger, which meant we could travel overseas. On the down side, no country with any real integrity would have us. Now that we are a democracy we can go anywhere we want, but can't afford it. Ironic, isn't it? It is almost as if the Illuminati are punishing us for achieving self-determination and nationhood.

I have a suggestion you may be interested in. Have you ever thought of getting the Mint to produce a 99 cent coin? You probably have someone to do your shopping for you, but you must have noticed that most things cost however many rand and 99 cents. Everything from ice creams to new cars end with 99 cents.

Some of us have amassed enromous quantities of one cent coins and we do not know what to do any more. Beggars won't take them and the banks are less than enthusiastic. A 99 cent coin will at least ensure that nobody will ever again be given one cent in change.

Obviously I understand the psychology behind pricing strategies. Manufacturers, entrepreneurs and other assorted free marketeers believe that consumers will be tricked into thinking they are getting a good deal on a new BMW that costs only R249 999,99. Make that same car R250 000 and he will immediately shy away. That's a quarter of a million rand! Far too expensive, he will say. And while he is thinking about his next move, he will buy a hamburger from a street vendor for R9,99 after threatening to sue a restaurant owner for extortion for daring to sell burgers at the exorbitant price of R10.

It follows that when you do introduce the 99 cent coin, the capitalists will end all their prices with 98 cents. And that is when you flood the market with 98 cent coins. They are then forced to drop to 97 cents, and you counter their move with a 97 cent coin. Do you see where this is going? Of course you do. You would not be the Governor of the Reserve Bank otherwise. The natural progression is that prices will keep plummeting as fast as the Mint can keep the coins coming.

This is the most revolutionary inflation-busting strategy ever devised. And to think I came up with it just a few minutes ago!

The inevitable outcome, of course, is that everything will eventually be free. Other governments will adopt the strategy and within a certain period of time (I tried to do the maths but my head began hurting) there will be no such thing as money anywhere in the world.

 I am prepared to let you claim the idea as your own, and I am enclosing R10 towards the awareness campaign. Let me know what else you need.

Yours truly,

Ben Trovato (Mr)

Mr Ben Trovato
PO Box 1117
Sea Point
8060

29 August, 2002

Dear Mr Mboweni,

I have not yet heard from you since I wrote on the 8th of August. I expect that your reply has gone missing in the mail.

You may recall that I provided you with a revolutionary inflation-busting idea that would simultaneously ensure that nobody would ever again be given one cent in change.

I also provided you with ten rand towards the cost of implementing this brilliant scheme. If you never received it, you might want to have a word with your secretary. Staff with sticky fingers should not be encouraged to work for the Reserve Bank.

I plan on being in Pretoria in the near future. If I do not hear from you within a couple of weeks, I will assume that you are interested in hearing more about my idea and shall stop by your office to brief you on the details.

Keep up the good work.

Yours truly,

....
Ben Trovato (Mr)

SOUTH AFRICAN RESERVE BANK

OFFICE OF THE GOVERNOR

18 September 2002

Dear Mr Trovato

Thank you very much for your letter of 8th August 2002. The contents thereof have been noted.

I think your idea of a 99 cent coin is worth looking at. I will ask the relevant people in the Bank to examine it.

Best wishes

TT MBOWENI
GOVERNER

The Manager
The Ice Station
GrandWest Casino
Vanguard Drive
Goodwood

Mr Ben Trovato
PO Box 1117
Sea Point
8060

13 August, 2002

Dear Sir,

I understand that the ice rink is available for private functions.

My wife and I are celebrating our wedding anniversary next month and we would like to book the rink for the evening. We intend inviting around fifty close friends, many of whom have skated before. One couple even lived in northern Sweden for several years, so ice is nothing unusual for them.

We would need your facility from 7pm to midnight. Do you handle catering or should everyone bring a bottle? Brenda says she can take care of the snacks if you are unable to provide something for our guests to nibble on.

Brenda and I are executive members of the Order of Spartacus, a close-knit fraternity of like-minded folk who hope to one day launch a rebellion against laws demanding that people wear clothes. Governments use the so-called 'public decency' clause as a tool of repression. Nudity is not indecent. It is a wonderful thing.

Most of the guests at our anniversary will be skating in the buff. I sincerely hope this will not be a problem. Please let me know what it will cost to hire the rink for five hours.

You are more than welcome to join us.

Looking forward to hearing from you.

Yours truly,

Ben Trovato (Mr)

GRANDWEST

• CASINO AND ENTERTAINMENT WORLD •

A division of SunWest International (Pty) Limited
1 Vanguard Drive Goodwood 7460
Tel: +27 (21) 505 7777

Company registration number: 1994/003869/07
P O Box 777 Eppindust 7475
Fax: +27 (21) 534 1278

6 September 2002

Dear Mr Trovato

50TH ANNIVERSARY

I refer to your recent letter with regards to the forthcoming visit of the Executive Committee of the Ancient Order of Frothblowers to GrandWest Casino & Entertainment World .

Could you please contact me on (021) 5057659 in order to schedule a meeting with the appropriate people involved, to ensure that your evening at GrandWest Casino is definitely one to remember.

Yours sincerely

MARINDA DE JONGH
PA TO THE GENERAL MANAGER, KURT PETER
GRANDWEST CASINO & ENTERTAINMENT WORLD

Mr Ben Trovato
PO Box 1117
Sea Point
8060
Cape Town

7 September, 2002

Dear Mr van Zyl,

I hear that you have an excellent track record when it comes to investigating crime.

To be honest, I don't take much notice of what goes on these days. The news is the same every day. In fact, the SABC would stand a far better chance of getting my attention if they started their bulletins with stories like "Mr John Adams of Rivonia has managed to get to work and back for six weeks in a row without once being threatened by hijackers or traffic police". Now, that would be news.

Most of the really good crimes have already been solved. That Englishman-cum-Boer and his Polish sidekick are doing time for murdering the communist Hani. Terreblanche is inside for sleeping with Jani Allen. Most of the Western Cape government is about to go to jail for accepting blood money from a man called Jurgen "Hans" Harksen.

There is one crime that has always intrigued me. Do you remember when a man called Anton Lubowski was murdered in Windhoek? I think it was in 1988 or 1989. Shot outside his home, if I recall correctly. If my memory serves me, there was an Irishman involved. But I think he got off and I never heard what happened after that.

Would you be interested in following this one up? My interest is purely academic, but I would be prepared to pay for small expenses like phone calls and parking.

Please let me know if you would like to take the case.

Yours truly,

Ben Trovato (Mr)

Mr Ben Trovato
PO Box 1117
Sea Point
8060

27 August, 2002

Dear Mr de Kock,

My wife, Brenda, and I invited the neighbours around for dinner the other night and we got to talking about you. Ted says that you have paid your dues and that you should be released, particularly since presidential pardons are being dished out to other murderers. Mary says you deserve your nickname 'Prime Evil' and should never be allowed on to the streets for as long as you live. They have that kind of marriage.

I am more interested in how you spend your days. Do you mix with the general population or have you asked to be kept apart from the natives? I am sure you have come into contact with prison gangs. Which group do you hang out with? With your reputation, I find it unlikely that you are some burly thug's bitch. Mary says you have probably aligned yourself with the white supremacists, but Ted feels it is unlikely that you need protection of any kind. Do you have gangs of Sharks supporters going up against Kaizer Chiefs fans, or is sport not really an issue on the inside? Brenda says she thinks you are divided along political lines. If so, where do you stand? Speaking of politicians, is there anything you would like to say to people like PW Botha and General Magnus Malan?

We were also wondering if anyone had approached you with regard to making a movie or writing a book about your life. Many high-profile celebrity convicts are easily bribed by Hollywood players, especially when they have nothing left to lose. This applies equally to the convicts and the players. The inmate sells the rights to his story, and then just before the switch is flicked he discovers that his life has been turned into an animated feature with Robin Williams doing his voice because a part of the company had to be sold off to Disney after the producer's cocaine habit hit the papers when he paid his lover's retarded brother to kill the dealer and take the rap. Don't let this happen to you.

I know you must be a busy man, but it would mean a lot if you took the trouble to reply. I have enclosed a stamped envelope in case stationery is hard to come by.

Yours truly,

Ben Trovato (Mr)

Mr Ben Trovato
PO Box 1117
Sea Point
8060

21 August, 2002

Dear Sir,

I have been meaning to write to you for a long time. My wife has now threatened to divorce me if I do not assert myself and claim what is rightfully mine.

Many years ago I had a friend who worked for Lever Brothers. He used to call me 'Skip' for reasons which need not be explained in this correspondence. We had a falling out when he attempted to seduce my Brenda after one too many tequila sunrises at my 40th birthday party. We have not seen one another since.

I cannot remember the precise date, but on a trip to my local supermarket I accidentally wandered into the aisle stocked with household detergents, disinfectants and other domestic products aimed at the female market. There, on the top shelf, was a product that bore my nickname. I was shocked. My estranged friend had clearly developed some sort of sanitising unguent and named it after me.

I obviously have copyright on the name Skip since my friends still call me this.

I have no objection if Lever continues to use the name. All I ask is fair compensation. I have done a quick calculation and you will be pleased to know that I am prepared to settle for R5 000 000 (five million rand).

Please send me a bank guaranteed cheque. Or I can provide you with my bank details and you can pop it straight into my account. Let me know which you prefer.

Let's get this settled!

Yours truly,

Ben 'Skip' Trovato

The Manager
SA Bullet Resistance Glass
PO Box 260254
Excom
2023

Mr Ben Trovato
PO Box 1117
Sea Point
8060

19 August 2002

Dear Sir,

My wife and I are firearm enthusiasts. We also have a fairly boisterous marriage. The two don't always go well together and there have been times in which Brenda and I have fought running gunbattles through the house. We never use anything bigger than .22 calibre weapons to avoid serious damage to the fittings. We also have an unspoken rule to never aim higher than the knees. I have found that kevlar padding absorbs most of the impact, although one is left with a nasty bruise for a few weeks afterwards.

Things have become a little hairy of late, and I need to order a fair amount of bullet resistant glass. The neighbours have threatened to have us arrested if another stray bullet lands up in their lounge wall. I expect the entire house will have to be refitted.

I need to know if bullets will ricochet off your special glass. This kind of information will give me an edge over Brenda as I could use the windows to deflect the ammunition without necessarily having to show myself. I need all the help I can get since her aim is better than mine and I frequently find myself at the losing end.

Please let me know what it would cost to fit a medium-sized window of about a metre square. I also have a bay window which will obviously be more expensive.

Please reply soon before there is a terrible accident.

Yours truly,

....
Ben Trovato (Mr)

PS. I know this is a long shot, but do you have any glass that is bullet resistant from one side, but can be penetrated from the other? If I could get some of that between me and Brenda I would certainly have the upper hand.

Mr Ben Trovato
PO Box 1117
Sea Point
8060

19 August 2002

Dear Sir,

My wife is planning a garden party early next month and wants to hire a dozen cranes to create a more elegant ambience. I suggested swans but Brenda said she was not prepared to risk having the guests being chased by enormous hissing creatures. She said cranes are well-behaved and inclined to keep to themselves. At worst, they are picky eaters.

I don't pretend to know my birds. In fact, I can't tell a crane from a flamingo. But my neighbour, Ted, tells me that cranes are aggressive birds that tend to sidle up to people and then with no warning at all will leap into the air and rake their unsuspecting victim with razor-sharp claws while stabbing at their eyes with a stiletto-like bill. He says they even give chase if their victim tries to run. This should certain liven up Brenda's soiree. I tried warning her but she called Ted an alarmist sociopath who should be put down.

Brenda says she would like to get a selection, if possible. She says blue cranes are very pretty. Maybe a few black necked cranes and one or two wattled cranes. I think it is best to stay away from whooping cranes. She does enough of that herself after a few brandies.

Brenda asks if you have a branch in Cape Town or would you have to ship them down? I suggested that it would be cheaper to fly them here, but they probably lack the instincts of a homing pigeon. I would hate to be responsible for losing a dozen of your best cranes.

Please give us a quote as soon as possible. A half day rate would be perfect for us.

Looking forward to doing business with you.

Yours truly,

....
Ben Trovato (Mr)

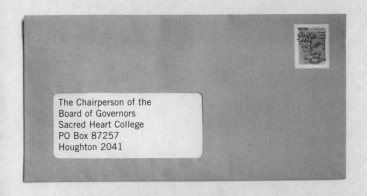

Mr Ben Trovato
PO Box 1117
Sea Point
8060

29 July, 2002

Dear Sir,

I understand that you are looking for someone to head up the college. Well, you need look no further. I am your man.

For a start, I would never allow that cross-dressing pervert Evita Peron to visit the school. We cannot have young Catholic minds tainted with degenerate displays of wanton licentiousness. Smut dressed up as education is like a wolf dressed up as lamb. And when Jesus Christ urged us to lie down with lambs, he meant us to keep our clothes on.

Your advertisement said the incumbent has accepted a similar challenge at another leading educational institution. However, my neighbour says this is Catholic code for "being transferred to a state facility" and that he is in all likelihood about to begin serving 20 years for getting a little too boisterous with the lads in the locker room. My neighbour is a Protestant, so I expect this kind of remark from him. I am sure the incumbent is a decent family man who is serious about his career.

I see that you need someone capable of "designing a pastoral care system appropriate to the South African context". Well, just off the top off my head, one word springs to mind. Cows. Very rural, very South African. They can graze on the rugby field, providing free fertilizer and keeping the grass neatly cropped. You do not get more pastoral than that.
This is just one idea. I have many more, not all involving animals.

Your advert also mentions that the school operates according to the charisma of the Marist Brothers. Nothing wrong with that. I think it is essential that we maintain a sense of humour in these terrible times. My personal favourite was Groucho, although I understand that as Head of College it will be expected of me not to show any bias. I can assure you of my impartiality at all times (except when I am alone in my room watching my personal copy of Duck Soup!).

I have many years of teaching experience, as you will see by my curriculum vitae which is in for repairs at the moment. I shall bring it along to the interview.

As you can see by my name, I am of fine Italian stock. And you do not get more Catholic than that. Just ask the pope! Enclosed please find a small donation to grease the wheels.

Yours truly,

....
Mr Ben Trovato

Mr Ben Trovato
PO Box 1117
Sea Point
8060

17 July, 2002

Dear Lady Thatcher,

You are one of the few genuine heroes of the 20th century.

What a tragedy that you were unable to stay in power for another 50 years. Unfortunately, you can only get away with that kind of thing in Africa. And even then you have to be a high-ranking military officer with reflecting sunglasses and a penchant for genocide.

We are fortunate to have a president who studied in Britain. He possesses a sophistication that is sadly lacking in other parts of Africa. Indeed, the entire country is fortunate that Britain once chose us to be part of its Empire. And many of us are grateful to this day.

My wife, Brenda, says it must be hard for you to live in a Britain run by that limp-wristed pantywaist, Tony Blair. She says if you ever decide to emigrate, you are more than welcome to stay with us. Now she has got me cleaning out the spare room just in case!

The natives are on strike at the moment. Well, just those who work for the municipalities. I can't say that I have noticed much change. There is endless bargaining and pleading for them to stop the strike. I wish we had you in charge! You would not hesitate to send in the horses, dogs and any other animals needed to drive them back to work.

Is there any chance of your son, Mark, going into politics? Britain could certainly do worse than have another Thatcher in No. 10. The Americans seem to have the knack of keeping it in the family.

Well, you must be very busy so I will say goodbye now. The spare room should be ready in a week or two, so please feel free to drop in. But give us some warning so that we can bribe the police to clean up the neighbourhood!

Please send our best regards to Denis.

Yours truly,

Ben Trovato (Mr)

Mr Ben Trovato
PO Box 1117
Sea Point
8060

17 July, 2002

Dear Sir or Madam,

I am hoping that you will be able to give me a little advice. I have a teenage son who has just returned home after spending some time at an institute for special children. Clive is very special. To Brenda and I, anyway.

Since he got back, he has shown considerable interest in acquiring pets. Not wanting to spark a relapse, we have given him most of the animals on his list. Except for the pangolin. I said to my wife, Brenda, that we already have a toothless, scaly, long-snouted mammal in the house. Hours later, when I was in the shower, she burst in and tried to kill me with the vacuum cleaner on full suck. She said she wanted to show me what an anteater is capable of doing. Luckily I managed to protect myself.

Clive now has a goldfish, two hamsters, a rabbit and a Pygmy Goat. The problem is that the lad has started training them. He seems to have some idea about starting his own circus. This is where I need your advice.

For the past few days, Clive has been trying to turn the hamsters into trapeze artists. He has constructed a small swing and a tightrope about a metre off the ground. The creatures seem to enjoy the trapeze because they grip tightly onto the swing and only let go when they are smacked sharply on the nose. But they are having trouble on the high wire. Their sense of balance is no good at all. I have tried to get Clive to put up a safety net, but he says that the only way they will learn is by hitting the floor. In your view, is this cruel or do you think these rodents have sufficient padding to cushion their fall?

Clive is also trying to teach the goldfish to jump through tiny hoops, much like a dolphin.
He says the only way you can train a goldfish is to take it out of the water for a minute or so every time it fails to perform. This is probably acceptable since fish have no feelings.

What worries me more are his attempts to get the rabbit and the goat to mate. Clive says he wants the progeny for his freak show. To be honest, the goat seems up for it. But the rabbit needs encouraging. I have tried telling Clive that electric shocks might not be the best method, but he says it worked at the institute. What is your opinion?

Give the operation a clean bill of health, and you are guest of honour at the first show!

Yours truly,

....
Ben Trovato (Mr)

Mr Ben Trovato
PO Box 1117
Sea Point
8060
Cape Town

17 July, 2002

Dear Mr Sirhan,

Greetings from South Africa.

My wife, Brenda, and I invited the neighbors around for dinner the other night and we got to talking about you. In fact, it all started with Bill Clinton and the haphazard manner in which he granted a bunch of pardons shortly before his term expired ahead of possible impeachment proceedings.

Not so haphazard, as it turned out. Some of the criminals who cracked the nod were either family, potential blackmailers, Hollywood players or prospective employers. But that's politics for you.

Why were you not on the list, Mr Sirhan? Did old Bill pass you by because you are not a Democrat? Actually, I have no idea where you stand politically, but I assume that since you killed Bobby Kennedy you were convicted under a Democratic administration. Any chance of parole now that the Republicans are back in office? After all, if it wasn't for people like you and Oswald, the Kennedys would have monopolized the White House for decades.

I understand that you were unable to remember shooting Kennedy. Did you ever get your memory back? The same thing happens to me occasionally, but my memory lapses are generally linked to Brenda pursuing me around the house demanding to know where I had been the night before. She won't stop until she gets an answer. It's like living with a prosecutor. I got home a little late the other night and the next day, while I was being interrogated, I tried telling her that I had been hypnotized early on in the evening. I told her that mind control is a powerful thing, and that she should not blame me for my actions. Needless to say, it did not work for me either.

We were wondering if you had many friends in Corcoran. Brenda says Charles Manson is bound to be a bad influence and that you should stay away from him. From what I have heard, Corcoran is not exactly a fun place to be. I read somewhere that there were forty inmate shootings between 1989 and 1995. It must be a bit like living in South Africa.

When you get released, you are welcome to come and stay with us for a while.

All the best.

Ben Trovato

Hon. Dr Manto Tshabalala-Msimang
Minister of Health
Private Bag X399
Pretoria
0001

Mr Ben Trovato
PO Box 1117
Sea Point
8060

14 July, 2002

Dear Minister,

Please allow me to commend you on the fine job you are doing. I thought you acquitted yourself particularly well at the recent Aids summit in Barcelona. My neighbour said he read somewhere that you had said you wanted to poison your people. This can't be right. I am sure you must have been misquoted. You know what these vultures in the media are like. The story was probably written inside an absinthe bar deep in the belly of the barrio chino, miles away from the conference centre. It has been shown that we cannot trust Spanish fishermen. Why should we trust their journalists?

But getting down to business. You are among the few truly honourable people left in politics. Your sense of compassion and justice frequently leaves me breathless. You run a corruption-free ministry and the health of the nation has never been better. Aids, after all, is not your fault.

As someone who has made it into my personal pantheon of political heroes, I would like to honour you by naming a new business venture after you. Manto's Nut Bar has a fine ring to it. You are probably asking, why nuts? Well, they are full of protein and a good quality nut is often hard to find these days. I plan on offering a range of dishes such as nut soufflés, nut curries, nut stews, nut soups, nut burgers, nut-based breakfast specials, nuts grilled, roasted, fried, boiled, curried and so on. Please could you provide me with a list of your favourite nuts, as I would like to name some of the dishes after you.

I was also hoping to cover the walls with a selection of photographs portraying highlights of your life. It would be wonderful if you included some from your childhood (although you might want to hold on to those showing little Manto at bath time!). Enclosed please find ten rand to cover postage costs.

I understand that in terms of the law, I am not obliged to seek permission to use your name in this manner. However, since I am your most ardent supporter, I thought you should be the first to hear about Manto's Nut Bar before the reviews start coming out. I am in the process of procuring a licence and hope that you will forward me the photographs and any other mementos I might be able to use.

Nuts to the people!

Yours truly,

Ben Trovato (Mr)

CASH GIVEN R10

197

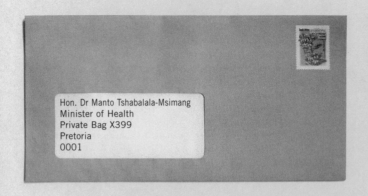

Hon. Dr Manto Tshabalala-Msimang
Minister of Health
Private Bag X399
Pretoria
0001

Mr Ben Trovato
PO Box 1117
Sea Point
8060

30 July, 2002

Dear Minister,

I have not yet had a response to my letter dated 14th July. I assume it went astray in the mail, since you are one of the few politicians who are on top of their game right now.

If you recall, I wrote to you informing you of my decision to name my new health bar after you.

I would also like to invite you to the opening of Manto's which I have scheduled for mid-October.

I also need to know if you are willing to send me mementoes of your life to use in a pastiche that I have planned for one of the walls. In my previous correspondence I enclosed ten rands towards postage costs. Did you receive it? Perhaps it was intercepted by a secretary afflicted with Boesakitis. Never mind, here is another. Let me know if you don't receive this one as well.

By the way, the opening will be informal so you might want to pick out something a little more frivolous than one of your parliamentary outfits.

Looking forward to hearing from you.

All the best.

Ben Trovato (Mr)

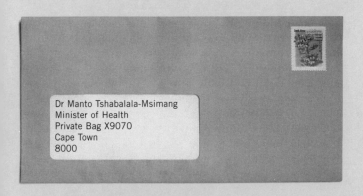

Dr Manto Tshabalala-Msimang
Minister of Health
Private Bag X9070
Cape Town
8000

Mr Ben Trovato
PO Box 1117
Sea Point
8060

23 August, 2002

Dear Minister,

I have not yet had a response to my letters dated 14th July and 7th August.

If you recall, I was enquiring about your availability to attend the opening of a new health bar that I have named in your honour.

I have already sent you R20 towards securing mementos from your life that I would like to use to decorate Manto's Nut Bar. Since I have not heard from you, I assume that you are waiting for more money. Enclosed please find another ten rand. This should do it.

Please let me know how you are placed for mid-October.

Looking forward to hearing from you.

All the best.

....
Ben Trovato (Mr)

CASH GIVEN
R10

Mr Ben Trovato
PO Box 1117
Sea Point
8060

5 June, 2002

Dear Sir,

My wife, Brenda, and I have been shopping around for an acceptable religion. We were going to become Catholics, but we were put off by the total lack of interest that the Church has with regard to winning converts. We also had a problem with the number of priests who have been caught up to their elbows in choirboys. It's not very nice.

If we are to become Scientologists, we need some assurances. Your leader, L. Ron Hubbard, has an interesting name and a quick mind when it comes to writing science fiction novels. But does he have what it takes to lead us out of this quagmire of confusion and into a quieter, gentler place? Is he a religious leader or a novelist? Is it possible to be both? I don't know of anyone else who has attempted to cover both angles. Many writers make the mistake of thinking that they are God, but their kind invariably end up dead in some or other mysterious love triangle involving cocaine and teenage girls from Cambodia. Can you assure us that Mr Hubbard is not that sort of leader?

I understand the Church deals with something called Dianetics. Brenda says it's to do with blood sugar levels and possibly the kidneys. Is she right? What do the kidneys have to do with religion? Is it because organs can be found in both the Church and the Body? Is that what you are saying? That the Church and the Body are indivisible? I can relate to that. Help us out here.

My neighbour, Ted, tells me that the American actor, Tom Cruise, is a Scientologist. That's no excuse for bad acting, as far as I'm concerned. Still, he's probably a good Scientologist, so it all balances out. On the other hand, I watched one of his movies the other day and distinctly remember seeing him put his tongue in a woman's mouth. I am pretty sure that she wasn't his wife. Mr Cruise also showed his bottom. Does the Church condone this kind of behaviour?

While we await your response, I plan on running a background check on the Hubbard fellow. If he comes up clean, then you can count us in. Let me know what it costs to join.

Yours truly,

....
Ben Trovato (Mr)

PS. Do you meet on Sundays, like the Christians?